W9-AON-343

Basics *of*
BUDDHISM
Key principles and how to practise

Pat Allwright

TAPLOW PRESS

Copyright © SGI-UK 1998

Reprinted 1999, 2000, 2002

All rights reserved

Published by

TAPLOW PRESS

An imprint of Soka Gakkai International of the United Kingdom

Taplow Court, Taplow, Buckinghamshire

This edition is sold subject to the condition that it shall not, by way of trade or otherwise, be lent, re-sold, hired out or otherwise circulated in any form of binding or cover other than that in which it is published, and without a similar condition being imposed on the subsequent purchaser.

A catalogue record for this book is available from the British Library.

ISBN 1 902056 00 0

Set in Bodoni and Univers

Printed and bound in the United Kingdom by Stanhope Press, London

Book design by Prue Bucknall

If you wish to free yourself from the sufferings of birth and death you have endured through eternity and attain supreme enlightement in this lifetime, you must awaken to the mystic truth which has always been within your life.

NICHIREN DAISHONIN

Contents

Foreword

The purpose of all Buddhist teachings is to enable human beings to overcome suffering and achieve happiness. A Buddha is an enlightened person; someone who is enlightened to the reality of life, who is in harmony with the rhythm of the universe, and who deeply understands the eternity of life. Although the enlightened state is very special, it is in no way superhuman. Buddhist teachings exist to lead people to find enlightenment for themselves.

Basics of Buddhism discusses concepts which are common to all schools of Buddhism. However, the interpretation of these differs markedly between schools. The interpretation here is from the viewpoint of Nichiren Daishonin's Buddhism. The book explains the fundamental philosophy, based on one of Nichiren Daishonin's first letters about his teachings, called 'On Attaining Buddhahood'. It also outlines the core of the practice. It concludes by explaining the role and purpose of the Soka Gakkai International (SGI), the worldwide movement dedicated to peace, culture and education based on Nichiren Daishonin's Buddhism.

Basics of Buddhism has been written so that each chapter is self-sufficient. It can be read in any order, or dipped into at random. Buddhism has many specialised words which have been kept to a minimum for ease of reading. Where these are unavoidable, an explanation can be found in a short glossary of terms at the end.

I am indebted to Barbara Cahill and Sue Craxton for the time and energy they have devoted to helping me in writing and editing this book. I am also grateful to Paul Williams for the production, Eddy Canfor-Dumas and Paul Miller for proof-reading, and Jean Kemble for researching the section on further reading. Thanks, most of all, to Daisaku Ikeda, whose prolific writings and speeches provide so much material on the content and spirit of this great philosophy of life. **Pat Allwright**

Introduction

O ver the centuries, our lifestyles have changed radically, and this is continuing at an increasing pace. Advances in technology mean that we have far less contact with the natural world than our ancestors, our involvement nowadays being mostly in a man-made society. Communications travel at the speed of light and, in this sense, our planet has shrunk to the size of a 'global village'. Less than one hundred years ago, hardly anyone owned a car and aeroplanes did not exist. Nowadays we can travel 12,000 miles, to the other side of the world, in less than a day.

Advances in technology were designed to make life easier, and therefore happier. Sadly, people are no happier than they were before. As the natural environment recedes at an alarming rate, so people's lives seem to match it in desertification. Unable to encompass the huge bombardment of information, people feel powerless and alienated. The age-old questions of 'why are we here and what is our purpose?' remain unanswered for most. Now, more than ever, we need to develop our inner human qualities to lend meaning to our lives.

The famous Greek adage exhorts us 'Know Thyself'. Surely this does not mean getting to know our limitations - what makes us angry, what makes us jealous or how long we need to sleep - which is what most people mean when they say, 'I think I know myself pretty well'. It must be referring to the enlightened qualities of humanity which exist in each one of us - such qualities as reason, wisdom, love for others, trust, courage and tolerance.

This being the case, Shakyamuni, the first historically recorded Buddha in India, would have agreed wholeheartedly with this adage. He attained enlightenment through introspection, realising the universal truth of all existence. This is the way of Buddhism - to seek our own enlightenment and find our own answers to the meaning of life.

In contrast to western religions, there is no concept of God in Buddhism. The word religion is generally understood as belief in a higher power. If this is so, Buddhism cannot be described as a religion at all. It is better described as a philosophy of life.

Buddhist concepts do not contradict common sense. In fact, Shakyamuni is reputed to have said, 'If it accords with reason, do it' and, 'If it works, do it'. Whether or not he actually said this, Buddhist teachings are essentially pragmatic. They accord with reason, observing life as it is, and propose a logical approach to life based on the true nature of existence.

In this country, people may have the impression that Buddhists observe many rules of behaviour, or practise only in monasteries. However, Nichiren Daishonin clarified that Buddhism *is* life. It is not necessary to seclude oneself, give up eating meat, wear robes or shave our heads. These were all practices adopted in much earlier times and in different countries. They were largely matters of practicality.

In fact, in Nichiren Daishonin's Buddhism, there are no rules of behaviour. Society has developed to the point where codes of behaviour are built into the system of justice. Buddhism is founded on the utmost respect for life. Given this, we decide for ourselves what is the best course of action, based on our own innate wisdom which arises and develops through practice.

Deep down, what really matters is that we feel connected: connected to ourselves, connected to others and connected to the universe. With reference to this, Daisaku Ikeda quotes psychiatrist Dr Joel Elkes of Johns Hopkins Hospital, Baltimore, USA:

> Healing is a restoration to the whole... the words healing, whole and holy, all derive from the same root. Holy is being complete, being connected as a person and with other persons, being connected with the planet. Pain is a signal that the part is separate from the whole.[1]

This throws new light on the word 'holy'. The desire for wholeness exists in all of us.

Buddhism observes that suffering results from seeing ourselves as individual entities independent of the universe as a whole. We think we are somehow separate, absolute and capable of living a self-orientated kind of life. The Buddhist doctrine of dependent origination clarifies that all life is interdependent, and that regarding oneself as separate is an illusion. Following on from this, frustration is the inevitable result of trying to cling on to things, to try to make them stay the same. Life is changing constantly. When our lives are in harmony with universal life, we can feel free to enjoy this change.

Buddhism is about becoming skilled in life. Change, troubled times and difficulty are inevitable. When we develop our inner strengths, we can enjoy these times as well as the moments of tranquillity. Enlightenment is not so much a goal, as a process.

Buddhahood is not so much a matter of arriving at a destination or reaching a goal, as internalising the process of continually strengthening the world of Buddhahood in our lives. This is termed 'entering the unsurpassed way'.[2]

Attaining Buddhahood is not a matter of 'becoming a Buddha', but of revealing what already exists within us. Buddhahood is not a superhuman state, but the process of developing our humanity.

The following chapters discuss some of the basic principles of Buddhism. Whether or not a person decides to practise Buddhism, the teachings provide a rational and humanistic philosophy to live by. People who hear about it for the first time often remark, 'I always thought that anyway'. This is because ultimately, we all know the universal truths, but have become separated from them. The adventure into the inner self is an endless journey of discovery, insight and joy.

A transformation in the inner reality of one's life, in one's mind, produces changes in the workings of one's life, in other people and also in the land.

A change in our determination first produces a change in the inner reaches of our lives; it enables us to manifest qualities of excellent health, abundant strength and boundless wisdom. A life that has been transformed in this way will lead others in the direction of happiness and be committed to overcoming suffering. It will also have an impact on society and the natural environment, transforming both into a paradise of peace and prosperity.[3]

1 Quoted in *A New Humanism*, p. 168.
2 Daisaku Ikeda, *Conversations & Lectures on the Lotus Sutra*, Vol. 3, p. 13.
3 Daisaku Ikeda, Speech given at Nagano, Japan on 6 August 1994. Printed in *SGI-UK Guidance Booklet*, Vol. 8, p. 50.

SPREAD OF BUDDHISM
DURING THE TWO THOUSAND YEARS
AFTER SHAKYAMUNI

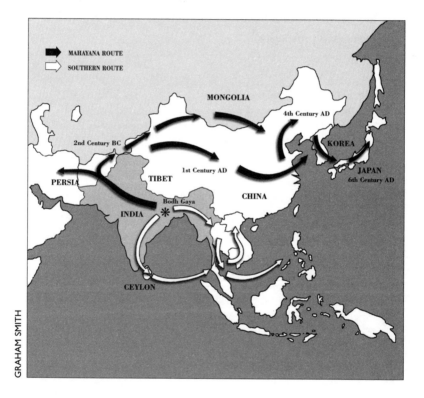

GRAHAM SMITH

A Short History of Buddhism

Shakyamuni, the first historically recorded Buddha, lived around three thousand years ago in India. He was born a prince, but renounced his secular life and devoted himself to finding a solution to the sufferings of birth, old age, sickness and death. He attained enlightenment through meditation and then taught for over forty years, according to the circumstances and understanding of the people he met. His teachings are therefore many and varied, and sometimes paradoxical.

In the last eight years of his life he gave his most profound teaching, the Lotus Sutra, despite the fact that he knew many people would not immediately understand it. When he taught this sutra, he urged his disciples to 'honestly discard expedient means'[1]. By this, he meant them to discard his previous teachings, which had been preparatory. This did not happen, partly because many of his followers did not understand, and partly because many had already departed and were spreading his earlier teachings.

This is why so many different forms of Buddhism exist today. Moreover, the teachings were added to, or modified, according to the culture and understanding of the people. This is only natural, since Buddhism is not a religion of dogma, but of action. It is a practical philosophy which relates to the time and place.

After Shakyamuni's death, Mahayana Buddhism[2] gradually spread to China, and from there, to Korea and Japan. This took place over a period of roughly one thousand five hundred years. During those periods when Buddhism flourished, peaceful and prosperous societies were established: in India during the reign of Ashoka the Great, China during the T'ang Dynasty and in Japan during the Heian period.

During the next five hundred years, established Buddhism started to decline. It had become formalised and ritualised so that only monks, or those with independent means, could undertake the lifetime of austerities involved. It had lost its effectiveness for ordinary people and it was now time for a revitalisation of the Buddhist teachings.

Shakyamuni had foretold this gradual decline and predicted the appearance of a Buddha who would reveal the correct teaching for the time beginning two thousand years after his death, which is known in Buddhism as the Latter Day of the Law. He also predicted the many persecutions this person would experience. Nichiren Daishonin underwent exactly these persecutions, and this is one of many specific reasons for calling him the Buddha of the Latter Day of the Law.

Nichiren Daishonin (Daishonin means great sage) was born in Japan in 1222. He was the son of a fisherman and was educated at a local temple, a common practice in those days. He chose to enter the priesthood and studied Buddhism widely before declaring, on 28 April 1253, that Nam-myoho-renge-kyo is the correct teaching for this time period.

Nichiren Daishonin spent the rest of his life expounding his teachings, teachings which enable ordinary people, living ordinary lives, to attain the same enlightened state as he did. On 12 October 1279, he inscribed his enlightened life-condition on a great mandala called the Dai-Gohonzon, dedicated to the happiness of all humankind.

Nichiren Daishonin declared that the Lotus Sutra is supreme amongst Buddhist teachings. This is mainly because of two points: it teaches that everyone without exception has Buddhahood, and it reveals that life is eternal. The Lotus Sutra describes the magnificence and wonder of life. However it is unlikely, were we to read it, that we would be able to understand it. The sutra was expounded at great length, using metaphors and parables. From his enlightened life-condition, Nichiren Daishonin was able to 'read between the lines' and declare the ultimate teaching.

Although Shakyamuni described the wondrous state of enlightenment, he did not define the fundamental law of the universe. Nichiren Daishonin revealed this Law as Nam-myoho-renge-kyo (see p.79) and taught a specific practice by which all people can attain enlightenment (see p.91).

Everything has its essential point and the heart of the Lotus Sutra is its title, Nam-myoho-renge-kyo... A law this easy to embrace and this easy to practise was taught for the sake of all mankind in this evil age of the Latter Day of the Law.[3]

1 *The Lotus Sutra* trans. Burton Watson, p. 44.

2 Mahayana literally means 'greater vehicle'. 'Vehicle' indicates a teaching or means to carry people to enlightenment. After Shakyamuni died, differences of opinion amongst his disciples led to two main streams: Mahayana, which stresses the importance of leading all people to enlightenment, and Theravada (later termed Hinayana, literally 'lesser vehicle', by Mahayana believers). The Theravadins held strictly to doctrine and ritual, as formulated for the monastic order. This stream spread mostly south and south-east of India to Sri Lanka, Burma and Thailand.

3 *The Major Writings of Nichiren Daishonin*, Vol. 1, p. 222.

On
Attaining
Buddhahood

Nichiren Daishonin wrote this letter in 1255, just two years after he had declared Nam-myoho-renge-kyo to be the ultimate Buddhist teaching. It was written to someone who had just started to practise Nichiren Daishonin's Buddhism and expresses the core of his teaching. It is printed in full here and phrases from it are explained in the chapters which follow.

If you wish to free yourself from the sufferings of birth and death you have endured through eternity and attain supreme enlightenment in this lifetime, you must awaken to the mystic truth which has always been within your life. This truth is Myoho-renge-kyo. Chanting Myoho-renge-kyo will therefore enable you to grasp the mystic truth within you. Myoho-renge-kyo is the king of sutras, flawless in both letter and principle. Its words are the reality of life, and the reality of life is the Mystic Law (*myoho*). It is called the Mystic Law because it explains the mutually inclusive relationship of life and all phenomena. That is why this sutra is the wisdom of all Buddhas.

Life at each moment encompasses both body and spirit and both self and environment of all sentient beings in every condition of life[1], as well as insentient beings - plants, sky and earth, on down to the most minute particles of dust. Life at each moment permeates the universe and is revealed in all phenomena. One awakened to this truth himself embodies this relationship. However, even though you chant and believe in Myoho-renge-kyo, if you think the Law is outside yourself, you are embracing not the Mystic Law but some inferior teaching. 'Inferior teachings' means those other than this sutra, which are all provisional and transient. No provisional teaching leads directly to enlightenment, and without the direct path to enlightenment you cannot attain Buddhahood, even if you practise lifetime after lifetime for countless aeons. Attaining Buddhahood in this lifetime is then impossible. Therefore, when you chant the Mystic Law and recite the Lotus Sutra, you must summon up deep conviction that Myoho-renge-kyo is your life itself.

You must never seek any of Shakyamuni's teachings or the Buddhas and bodhisattvas of the universe outside yourself. Your mastery of the Buddhist teachings will not relieve you of mortal sufferings in the least unless you perceive the nature of your own life. If you seek enlightenment outside yourself, any discipline or good deed will be meaningless. For example, a poor man cannot earn a penny just by counting his neighbour's wealth, even if he does so night and day. That is why Miao-lo states, 'Unless one perceives the nature of his life, he cannot eradicate his evil karma.'[2] He means here that unless one perceives the nature of his life, his practice will become an endless, painful austerity. Miao-lo therefore condemns such students of Buddhism as non-Buddhist. He refers to the passage in the *Maka Shikan*, 'Although they study Buddhism, their views revert to those of non-Buddhists.'

Whether you chant the Buddha's name,[3] recite the sutra or merely offer flowers and incense, all your virtuous acts will implant benefits and good fortune in your life. With this conviction you should put your faith into practice. For example, the *Jomyo* Sutra says the Buddha's enlightenment is to be found in human life, thus showing that common mortals can attain Buddhahood and that the sufferings of birth and death can be transformed into nirvana. It further states that if the minds of the people are impure, their land is also impure, but if their minds are pure, so is their land. There are not two lands, pure or impure in themselves. The difference lies solely in the good or evil of our minds.

It is the same with a Buddha and a common mortal. While deluded, one is called a common mortal, but once enlightened, he is called a Buddha. Even a tarnished mirror will shine like a jewel if it is polished. A mind which presently is clouded by illusions originating from the innate darkness of life is like a tarnished mirror, but once it is polished it will become clear, reflecting the enlightenment of immutable truth. Arouse deep faith and polish your mirror night and day. How should you polish it? Only by chanting Nam-myoho-renge-kyo.

What then does *myo* signify? It is simply the mysterious nature of our lives from moment to moment, which the mind cannot comprehend nor words express. When you look into your own mind at any moment, you perceive neither colour nor form to verify that it exists. Yet you still cannot say it does not exist, for many differing thoughts continually occur to you. Life is indeed an elusive reality that transcends both the words and concepts of existence and non-existence. It is neither existence nor non-existence, yet exhibits the qualities of both. It is the mystic entity of the middle way that is the reality of all things. *Myo* is the name given to the mystic nature of life, and *ho* to its manifestations.

Renge, the lotus flower, symbolises the wonder of this Law. Once you realise that your own life is the Mystic Law, you will realise that so are the lives of all others. That realisation is the mystic *kyo*, or sutra. It is the king of sutras, the direct path to enlightenment, for it explains that the entity of our minds, from which spring both good and evil, is in fact the entity of the Mystic Law. If you have deep faith in this truth and chant Myoho-renge-kyo, you are certain to attain Buddhahood in this lifetime. That is why the sutra states, 'After my death, you must embrace this sutra. Those who do so shall travel the straight road to Buddhahood.'[4] Never doubt in the slightest, but keep your faith and attain enlightenment in this lifetime. Nam-myoho-renge-kyo, Nam-myoho-renge-kyo.

Respectfully,
Nichiren [5]

1 In every condition of life: In any of the ten states of life.
2 *Maka Shikan Bugyoden Guketsu*, Vol. 4.
3 Buddha's name: As used here, it denotes Nam-myoho-renge-kyo.
4 *Lotus Sutra*, chap. 21.
5 *The Major Writings of Nichiren Daishonin*, Vol. 1, pp. 3-5.

Ten States *of* Life

*'While deluded, one is called
a common mortal,
but once enlightened,
he is called a
Buddha.'*

Life changes from moment to moment. You may wake up feeling good, go into the kitchen and find a sink full of washing-up. Instantly you feel irritated; you can't get the kettle under the tap. After a strong cup of coffee, your spirits somewhat restored, a cheque you had been waiting for arrives in the post. You feel even better, but a hold-up on the way to work makes you feel anxious about being late.

At work, how you feel and act changes according to what is demanded of you, how well you are able to respond to those demands, and the moods of everyone else. If you have a bad day, a couple of drinks after work may induce a sense of euphoria, which vanishes when you realise there is no food at home and you are going to have to battle through the supermarket, or get yet another expensive take-away. Once home and able to relax, you may forget all the worries of the day and feel calm again.

Our lives are constantly changing. The changing conditions which we experience are defined in Buddhism by ten states of life (often called the ten worlds). We can all recognise these life-states, although our experience of them may differ according to our individual personalities. Each state describes a common way of experiencing life from moment to moment. We change from one to the other all the time, although we may identify some that we experience more often than others.

Hell: extremity of suffering

This is a state of abject misery. In this condition one feels continuous torment and anguish. One feels trapped and powerless, as if in prison. This feeling of helplessness induces the anger of frustration. It is a different kind of anger from that of, for example, anger for justice. It is helpless rage. In hell, time seems painfully slow. Space, or one's sphere of influence, is severely restricted. For example, when we are depressed we can think of nothing but ourselves, and we feel as if our depression will last for ever.

Hunger: insatiable desire

Hunger is characterised by greed. Desires dominate one's life. Even if a desire is satisfied, one is only temporarily appeased before being dominated by another desire. Of course, like any other of the ten states, desire is essential to life. Desire has been the driving force behind civilisation and has brought about many improvements. However, if desire is unchecked by respect and wisdom, it becomes selfish greed which leads to destruction, as evidenced by pollution.

Animality: a life of instinct

In this state, one follows one's instinctive desires with no thought of the outcome. It is called animality because it is like the law of the jungle, where the strong prey upon the weak and the weak fear the strong. It is natural in the animal world for hunters to kill the weakest of their prey, which in turn helps to preserve the strength of that species. Self-preservation, such as getting enough food and sleep, is a vital function of animality. However, instinct needs to be tempered by the human qualities of reason, conscience, love and mercy. If it is not, we will be unable to create and maintain a peaceful and constructive co-existence in both our personal lives and the world at large.

Conditions of suffering

The life-conditions of hell, hunger and animality are collectively called the three evil paths. They are called evil because they are conditions of suffering in which one is controlled by helpless agony, desire or other instinctive forms of behaviour. The fourth state, anger, does have an element of humanity in that one is self-conscious and consequently aware of the opinion of others. Nevertheless, it too is a state of suffering. Anger is therefore grouped with hell, hunger and animality, which together form the four evil paths.

Anger: the world of conflict

A person in anger is dominated by ego. He thinks he is better, and knows better, than everyone else, and works exclusively for his own benefit. Concerned about the opinion of others, he may make an outward show of being benevolent or righteous, but inwardly he is solely motivated by his own gain.

The anger of this state is different to the self-consuming rage of hell. In anger, one's conceit and desire to win is paramount, so the anger is directed outwards. As opposed to the rage of hell, which is debilitating, this kind of self-righteous anger has tremendous energy which can also be used in creative ways, such as in defending a just cause.

Tranquillity: the human being

In tranquillity, one controls his instinctive desires with reason. This is the humane, calm and reasonable state of mind in which one is at peace with himself and others. It has such qualities as intelligence, sound judgement, superior wisdom, the ability to distinguish truth from falsehood, and a good temperament. Although tranquillity, also called humanity, is the state which is most natural to human beings, it is not easy to maintain in our turbulent society.

Rapture: overwhelming joy

Rapture, sometimes called heaven, is the exhilaration experienced through the satisfaction of a desire. This state is sub-divided into the worlds of desire, form and formlessness. In the first of these, rapture comes from the satisfaction of any desire, such as eating one's favourite food, gaining a material possession, or achieving power or recognition. Rapture in the world of form has to do with physical well-being and energy, such as the pleasure derived from sex or the exhilaration of sport. In the world of formlessness, it is the spiritual fulfilment of intense creativity.

In rapture, time flies past and one has a strong influence on the outer world. One feels light, filled with energy and tremendously joyful. However, this state is short-lived. Once the desired objective palls, one tends to fall into hunger, hell or animality.

Learning: self-reflection

The last four of the ten states are termed the four noble paths because in order to experience them, one has to make an effort. In the six lower life-states, one wanders weakly from state to state, depending on changing circumstances. To experience the four noble paths, one must make a conscious effort to motivate and direct one's life. In the state of learning one has an open mind, applies oneself to self-development through learning from others, and gains wisdom through self-reflection. A person in this state is actively looking for deeper meaning in life.

Absorption: realisation

Absorption is very similar to learning in that one is seeking to cultivate oneself. However, rather than learning from others, one gains insight and wisdom from introspection and intuition. A classic example of a person in absorption is Archimedes who, it is popularly believed, shouted 'Eureka!' when he realised his famous principle whilst musing in the bath. This life-state is very creative and absorbing, hence its name.

Literature, music and the arts, as well as the great discoveries of science, stem from the states of learning and absorption. Whilst often motivated by concern for the welfare of others, those dominated by these states can tend to be inward-looking. They can become oblivious to others and lose sight of the possible effects of their great discoveries and inventions until it is too late. An outstanding example of this is the development of the nuclear bomb. A more personal example might be an artist who, absorbed in his work, fails to take care of his family.

Learning and absorption are known jointly as the two vehicles.

People who are inclined towards these life-states often attain positions of prominence in society and can therefore have far-reaching influence. However, those who have mastered a great deal of theory may adopt a superior attitude, thinking they know it all. If this happens, they lose the will to develop themselves, become arrogant and selfish, and fall back into one of the six lower states, such as anger or animality.

Bodhisattva: caring for others

One experiences this state when devoted to helping others. The great compassion of the state of bodhisattva is seen in the most caring nurses, doctors and teachers who are dedicated to the welfare of others, even at the expense of their own comfort. Mothers too, who show unconditional love for their children, are in this state. The negative aspect of this life condition is that those devoted to caring for others often wear themselves out in the process, having no way of replenishing their energy. This has become known as 'compassion fatigue'.

Bodhisattva originally meant one who summons up courage in the hope of attaining Buddhahood. In a Buddhist sense, therefore, in the state of bodhisattva one recognises that helping others is the most effective way of perfecting oneself. Empathising with another's suffering, one takes action to help, thereby overcoming selfish and egotistical tendencies. In Nichiren Daishonin's Buddhism, therefore, the bodhisattva is not selfless. The development of the self - that is, the greater self of reason, conscience, wisdom and courage - is vitally important in order to release the limitless energy of compassion from within. Self-reformation and altruism go hand in hand so that one does not yield to the weaknesses of despair, selfishness or ego.

Bodhisattvas of the Earth

Nichiren Daishonin often referred to his followers as Bodhisattvas of the Earth. First described in the fifteenth chapter of the Lotus Sutra, they appeared from the earth to spread the Buddhist Law throughout the universe. The earth symbolises that these are ordinary people, from every walk of life, who choose to devote themselves to working for the good of all. Earth also means the foundation of Buddhahood.

Bodhisattvas of the Earth have four virtues: true self, eternity, purity and happiness. These are developed through self-reformation. The virtue of true self is established by strengthening oneself to withstand difficulties, turning them into opportunities for growth. The virtue of eternity is to experience freedom, through believing in the eternity of life, and to work spontaneously towards the greater happiness of society. Purity is to demonstrate true wisdom and reason, unswayed by selfish desires or ego. Happiness means to live with great joy, securely founded on the creative power of life. These qualities are developed by tapping into the 'earth' of Buddhahood. Bodhisattvas of the Earth are truly humane, compassionate and joyful people.

Buddhahood: the state of enlightenment

Many people may think that Buddhahood is a kind of superhuman state which has only been attained by one person: the Buddha. However, 'Buddha' means an enlightened person. It is indeed an unsurpassed state of life and, in Nichiren Daishonin's Buddhism, it is accessible to all.

Although the Lotus Sutra taught that all people are equally capable of attaining Buddhahood, it did not teach a means whereby everyone could actually do so. Nichiren Daishonin defined the Law of the universe, or the Law of life, as Nam-myoho-renge-kyo (see p.79), so that we can actually harmonise our lives with the universe. This generates understanding of the continuity of past, present and future: the eternity of life. It gives direct access to the boundless life-force of the cosmos, as well as the great wisdom which arises from being in oneness with all life. The essential nature of the universe is compassion, so that in Buddhahood one's main concern is to save all life from suffering.

Buddhist teachings traditionally portray the Buddha as an incredible being with mystic powers. Nichiren Daishonin clarifies that these are descriptions of the magnificence of human life or, more broadly speaking, all life, including insentient life. However, from a personal point of view, the important revelation is that each one of us has unlimited potential and power to overcome suffering and live based on indestructible happiness. Nichiren Daishonin says:

> You, yourself, are a true Buddha who possesses the three enlightened properties [courage, wisdom and compassion]. You should chant Nam-myoho-renge-kyo with this conviction.[1]

The people of thirteenth century Japan thought the Buddha was a being with superhuman powers: something they could never aspire to. Nichiren Daishonin therefore often encouraged his followers by reassuring them, as well as us, that Buddhism is about how to fulfil the whole of our potential as human beings, overcome suffering, be happy, and help others.

TEN STATES OF LIFE

BUDDHAHOOD	enlightenment
BODHISATTVA	caring for others
ABSORPTION	realisation
LEARNING	self-reflection
RAPTURE	heaven
TRANQUILLITY	humanity
ANGER	self-righteousness
ANIMALITY	instinctive behaviour
HUNGER	greed
HELL	extreme suffering

The mutual possession of the ten states

In early Buddhist teachings, the above ten states were thought to exist in separate places. This is why they were called the ten worlds. It was considered impossible to move from one world to another within a single lifetime. There are still some Buddhist sects which sustain the belief that a 'pure land' (rapture or heaven) can be attained only after death, and that one must therefore endure suffering and devote oneself to good deeds in order to be reborn there. Endurance and perseverance are undoubtedly admirable human qualities. However, religions which teach that a 'pure land' lies elsewhere leave people open to exploitation, keeping them in their place, working hard and expecting nothing, in the hope of a better life after death.

In contrast, Nichiren Daishonin's Buddhism teaches the mutual possession of the ten states: each state contains all ten within itself. This means that all people, whatever their life-state, have the potential to reveal Buddhahood. Also, very importantly, it means that the Buddha state is not removed from ordinary life because it contains all ten states. In other words, there is no separation between a Buddha and an ordinary person. Buddhahood is accessible to anyone and everyone.

People in the state of Buddhahood then, do not cut themselves off from the realities of daily life in the nine worlds. Because their lives have a secure foundation, they actively delve into society in order to help others. In this way, they are able to reveal the creative qualities of the nine states. Everything becomes a source of growth. The suffering of hell becomes a means to empathise with others. Hunger becomes desire for peace. Animality promotes gratitude for others' support. Anger becomes anger for justice, and so on.

Buddhahood is endowed with infinite compassion and wisdom. The wisdom of Buddhahood penetrates to the diabolic nature that subverts life and tries to destroy it. The compassion of Buddhahood furnishes the energy to overcome this evil force.

In this way, the wisdom and compassion of Buddhahood become manifest in the nine states. And as they act in these states, they themselves are nourished and increased, strengthening the Buddhahood within us.

We must not, for this reason, seek to avoid the difficulties and challenges of the nine states, but rather meet them head on and overcome them, thus turning them into valuable experience. If one attempts to avoid difficulties, one misses the chance to develop and improve oneself. To avoid trouble is no more than to succumb to the illusions of the nine states. The mark of Buddhahood is the ability to meet all challenges and turn them into good. Indeed, the person who bases his life on Buddhahood seeks out new difficulties and new challenges that need to be overcome for the sake of the world, as well as for his own growth and development.[2]

1 *The Major Writings of Nichiren Daishonin*, Vol. 1, p. 30.
2 Daisaku Ikeda, *Life: An Enigma, a Precious Jewel*, pp. 144-5.

Cause *and* Effect

'Renge, the lotus flower, symbolises the wonder of this Law. Once you realise that your own life is the Mystic Law, you will realise that so are the lives of all others.'

The future is unknown. What is our destiny and what causes it? Some people believe that it is influenced by the stars, some that it is a matter of chance. Others think that fate is not ours to question. Whatever we choose to believe, anxiety is caused by uncertainty about the future.

Everyone wants to live a long, healthy and fulfilled life. It is very difficult to do this if we do not have an understanding of how destiny is created. Much as we may try to improve our circumstances, an unexpected misfortune can throw us off course. This makes us feel as if we are being carried along by our changing destiny, like flotsam and jetsam on the currents of the ocean.

Buddhism explains destiny through the concept of karma. Karma originally meant action. Later, it came to be understood as the destiny one had created through these actions. Every thought, word and deed is a cause which creates an effect. On a simple level, if we go to work, we will get paid. If we exercise, we will become fit. Buddhism therefore teaches that our fate is not arbitrary, neither is it imposed by supernatural forces. We create our own destiny:

> If you want to understand the causes that existed in the past, look at the results as they are manifested in the present. And if you want to understand what results will be manifested in the future, look at the causes that exist in the present.[1]

The workings of cause and effect may not be immediately obvious. Very often life seems unfair. How is it that an unscrupulous and selfish businessman can become so rich? Why is it that the nice woman down the road has cancer? Why are people born in such different circumstances? Surely a child has had no chance to make the causes to be born into poverty and hunger?

The concept of karma is based on the understanding that life is eternal (see p.73). Circumstances of birth are therefore determined by causes made in previous lifetimes. The law of cause and effect is exact. We may be able to escape detection from the laws of society but there is no escaping this law of causality, which is etched indelibly in our lives. Although it is strict, it cannot be said to be unjust. It certainly gives a logical explanation for our differing circumstances of birth. Furthermore, it is an optimistic teaching, because the power to create our destiny lies in our own hands.

On its face value, the law of causality may sound moralistic, but it is much more complex than a straight moral code. Science, of course, recognises cause and effect. However, science has discovered that the effect of a cause cannot be predetermined: the effect of a particular cause depends on the influence of many other factors. In a similar way, we cannot say that the nice woman down the road getting cancer is a result of her being a terrible person. It may be that she is very caring and helps others, but she is also extremely worried and, in her case, this unease of mind and body has manifested itself as cancer.

It is impossible, also, to look at effects and label them as good or bad. Some people who discover they have cancer develop a fighting spirit and a new appreciation of life. These people are truly creating their own destiny, through their spirit to live now and for the future. This is the spirit of Nichiren Daishonin's Buddhism.

In the West, we may have received the impression that karma is fatalistic and fixed. However, the reverse is true. Because we take full responsibility for our own actions, and therefore our own results, we are empowered to seize our own destiny and change it for the better.

The nine consciousnesses

Buddhism defines nine layers of consciousness. This doctrine helps to explain how karma is stored and how it can be changed. The first five consciousnesses are the five senses of sight, hearing, touch, taste and smell. The sixth level is the thinking mind which integrates the information we receive from these five senses. For instance, when you see a rose in blossom and smell its fragrance, your sixth sense integrates what you have seen and smelt to identify it as a rose.

The seventh consciousness is where we form judgements about what action to take. It corresponds to the thinking and aware self which

THE NINE CONSCIOUSNESSES

1-5	THE FIVE SENSES - EYES, EARS, NOSE, MOUTH, SKIN
6	INTEGRATION OF SENSES - REASON AND LOGIC
7	ABSTRACT OR SPIRITUAL THOUGHT, SELF-AWARENESS & INTUITION
8	STOREHOUSE OF KARMA
9	FUNDAMENTAL PURE CONSCIOUSNESS - BUDDHAHOOD

discerns value. 'Shall I pick this rose?' you think. 'No, better not, it's in someone else's garden.' This seventh level is the area of motivation and intention, much of it subconscious.

The eighth (*alaya*) consciousness is the storehouse of our karma. *Alaya* literally means 'accumulation', as in the name Himalaya mountains which means 'accumulation of snow'. All of our experiences are filtered through the initial seven layers of consciousness and stored in the eighth, which exists as an unconscious memory of all our previous actions and reactions. This influences our reactions at any given time, based on our past experiences, including those of previous lifetimes.

You may recognize repetitive patterns in your behaviour. You may find, for instance, that someone at work always makes you angry. Much as you reflect and determine that next time it happens you will rise above it, you find that you are stuck in the same pattern of behaviour. Or you may find that after having had an unhappy relationship, you get together with a new partner, but that soon the same problems start to occur in the new relationship. These kinds of behavioural patterns are all included in karma.

These patterns of behaviour are also perpetuated in family groups. People whose karma is similar are drawn together in families. For example, research has shown that children who are abused are, in turn, more likely to abuse their own children. On the face of it, one would think that a person who has suffered abuse is the least likely person to abuse others. The doctrine of karma clarifies why it is that people behave in these repeating cycles.

Psychology recognises the existence of conditioned responses such as are stored in the eighth consciousness and seeks to help people change these through understanding or self-awareness. Although it undoubtedly helps to understand our behaviour with our rational minds, our most deeply ingrained karma cannot be changed in this way, because the eighth consciousness lies deeper than the rational mind (seventh consciousness). Our thoughts are therefore constantly influenced by our karma.

In order to change karma fundamentally, we have to get beyond its influence into the realm of the ninth consciousness, which is pure and undefiled, free of karmic impurities. Nichiren Daishonin defined the ninth consciousness as Nam-myoho-renge-kyo, the universal law of life. When we chant Nam-myoho-renge-kyo, we are expressing our Buddhahood. As we do this more and more, we become aware of those karmic tendencies which are restricting us. As our confidence grows, we feel able to challenge these tendencies and establish a new direction in our lives, based on our ever-emerging Buddhahood.

The Buddha discovered a mystic law which simultaneously contains cause and effect, and designated it as *myoho-renge*. The single law of *myoho-renge* is perfectly endowed with all phenomena in the universe. Therefore, those who practise this law simultaneously acquire the cause and effect of Buddhahood.[2]

Cause and effect are simultaneous

Nichiren Daishonin taught that negative karma can be overcome in this lifetime, overturning the traditional belief that this would take many lifetimes. He revealed the simultaneity of cause and effect as expressed in *renge*, of Nam-myoho-renge-kyo.

Renge means lotus flower. The lotus flower produces flowers and seeds at the same time, indicating that the effect is simultaneous with the cause. Again, this can be difficult to understand, because we see cases such as a rich man who got where he is by stepping on other people, seemingly escaping cause and effect. To this, Nichiren Daishonin says:

> The reason I see it this way is that hell is in the heart of a man who inwardly despises his father and disregards his mother, just like the lotus seed, which contains both flower and fruit at the same time. In the same way, the Buddha dwells inside our hearts.[3]

True happiness depends on what is in our hearts. No matter what we may gain materially from manipulating others, if we are hating or disrespecting them, then *at that moment* we are suffering, as well as making the cause to suffer in the future.

Buddhist theory explains that there are actually two effects, one of which is invisible and one which is visible. The visible effect, called the manifest effect, may take time to appear. However, the invisible, or latent effect, is felt immediately. So in the case of the rich man who is misusing others, the manifest effect may take time to appear. He may, for instance, be born into a poor family in his next lifetime. However, the internal effect is immediate: inside he is suffering deeply.

Just as there are two effects, there are two causes. One is internal and arises from our karma; the other is external. External causes are everyday events which each of us respond to differently, depending on our own particular internal cause, stored in our karma. For example, an angry person will always tend to react hastily and irritably. However, if we base ourselves on the Buddha state, the ninth consciousness, our responses are not conditioned by our karma and we can break free of our habits and past conditioning. Josei Toda, the second president of the Soka Gakkai (see p.108) said:

> We common mortals need a supreme law which will enable us to break through the shell of the more immediate causes and effects and open the Buddha nature innate within us. It is Nichiren Daishonin who, responding to this need, established the law with which we, while leading our everyday lives, can demolish the

destiny which has continued from our past existences and rebuild it for the better... Devoting oneself to the Gohonzon [see p.85] and chanting Nam-myoho-renge-kyo [see p.79] is the way to change one's destiny for the better. All the causes and effects in between disappear, and the common mortal since time without beginning emerges.[4]

The implication of the doctrine of karma is that we cannot blame anyone else for our suffering. Of course this does not mean that others are not accountable; they will reap the rewards of their own actions. The important point is that our suffering comes from inside us, not outside. Again, this may seem strict, but in fact it is extremely liberating. After all, we cannot change other people. Or rather, the only way we can change other people is to change the way we relate to them, by first of all changing ourselves. When we open our Buddha nature through chanting Nam-myoho-renge-kyo, we react differently to others, based on wisdom and compassion rather than anger or greed. Because of this, people respond to us differently.

When we practise Nichiren Daishonin's Buddhism, there are no stages to go through. We can experience Buddhahood immediately because of the simultaneity of cause and effect, as expressed in *renge* of Nam-myoho-renge-kyo. Although, as explained above, it may take time for the external effect to appear - to overcome poverty or illness, for example - we can feel supreme joy immediately. This kind of joy is profoundly different to the satisfaction of physical desires; it is the joy of freedom. At the same time, we can also be sure that our physical and material circumstances will improve.

This does not mean that when we practise we avoid the effects of our karma. In fact, we find that those hidden things that cause us to suffer start to surface. This means we are changing them. They surface because we are tapping into the ninth consciousness, underneath the storehouse of karma. The flaws have to come to the surface in order to be purified, as in the process of forging iron. This can be quite unsettling and sometimes very difficult. There is, however, no such thing as karma which cannot be overcome.

At difficult times when we are wrestling with the effects our karma, it is important to remember that the causes we made in the past are not important. Rather, what we are doing now is creating the best possible causes for the future. Practising Nichiren Daishonin's Buddhism makes us much stronger and better able to deal with difficulties. Furthermore, we feel both joy and gratitude because we are able to revolutionise our lives fundamentally.

Karma is not a matter of oneself alone. As well as individual karma, we also share karma with our families. Likewise, we share it with our communities and society at large. There have been many attempts to improve society through various revolutions: the industrial revolution, the class revolution and so on. However, unless we have a way to achieve a revolution in our own lives, we cannot hope to achieve lasting peace and a constructive society. Unless we can overcome our own anger, for instance, how can we hope to stop war? In overcoming our own karma, therefore, we start a chain reaction to change the karma of our families, communities and the world.

We, living beings, have dwelt in the sea of the sufferings of birth and death since time without beginning. But now that we have become votaries of the Lotus Sutra, we will without fail attain the Buddha's entity which is as indestructible as a diamond, realising that our bodies and minds that have existed since the beginningless past are inherently endowed with the eternally unchanging nature, and thus awakening to our mystic reality with our mystic wisdom.[5]

1 *The Major Writings of Nichiren Daishonin*, Vol. 2, p. 172.

2 *Major Writings*, Vol. 7, pp. 65-6.

(The translation here has been simplified for ease of understanding).

3 *Major Writings*, Vol. 1, p. 271.

4 *Toda Josei Zenshu* (The Collected Works of Josei Toda), Vol. 3, p. 394.

5 *Major Writings*, Vol. 2, pp. 55-6.

Transforming
Suffering
and
Illusion

'...the Buddha's enlightenment is to be found in human life, thus showing that common mortals can attain Buddhahood and that the sufferings of birth and death can be transformed into nirvana.'

Shakyamuni, the historical founder of Buddhism, was born as a prince of the Shakya tribe in northern India. The date of his birth is unknown, but it is generally believed to have been sometime between the fourth and fifth century BC. It seems he was a sensitive and philosophical young man who, even though he was surrounded by luxury, could not reconcile himself to living a purely secular life.

The young prince was shielded from reality within the confines of the palace. Historical records about his life are scanty, but it is said that occasionally he managed to venture forth from this protective environment. One day he left by the eastern gate and was moved by the appearance of an old man. On another occasion he emerged from the south gate where he saw a sick man and on leaving by the west gate, he witnessed a corpse. Finally he went out of the north gate and was deeply impressed by a religious man who was passing by. It is believed that these events led Shakyamuni to renounce his throne and take up the religious life himself in order to find the solution to the four kinds of suffering: birth, old age, sickness and death.

While this story is no doubt symbolic, it focuses on the reason for the birth of Buddhism: the search for a solution to the problem of human suffering. Of course, this search is not limited to Buddhism alone; all religions and philosophies aim to solve this question. Indeed, Plato said that philosophy is an exercise in understanding death.

Death is inescapable, yet many people concentrate their lives on amassing wealth and fortune, ignoring this most fundamental of human dilemmas. We are able to feel completely secure only when we have reached an understanding of the true nature of life and death. Without such an understanding, ultimately our lives seem empty and futile and we are prone to fear. Finding the solution to the four sufferings is crucial to our well-being.

Early Buddhist teachings, recognising that suffering is inherent in life, arrived at the conclusion that the way to overcome suffering was to reach a state whereby one could escape the cycle of birth and death. This is the original meaning of the word nirvana, literally 'blown out'.

Many people still have the impression that all Buddhists are attempting to achieve this state. There are also many other religions in existence which teach that true happiness or fulfilment lies after death.

Nichiren Daishonin however, asserted that happiness does not lie in some far away place. Rather, enlightenment can be achieved in the midst of the reality of daily life. Nirvana, in terms of Nichiren Daishonin's Buddhism, therefore means to attain enlightenment while undergoing the cycle of birth and death and living in ordinary society.

Buddhism teaches that suffering is caused by illusions, instinctive desires and negative impulses which are inherent in human life. There are many definitions of these to the extent of 'illusions as innumerable as particles of dust and sand'. They are usually collectively referred to in English as 'earthly desires'. However, this translation can be misleading, since they include hatred, arrogance, inherent distrust and fear as well as insatiable desire and short-term gratification. In short, they consist of anything which causes us to suffer physically or spiritually and obstructs our attainment of enlightenment. 'Deluded impulses' is perhaps a better way to describe such illusions, which motivate us to take actions which result in suffering.

Fundamentally, anger, greed and ignorance are at the root of all suffering. They are known collectively as the 'three poisons'. For example, anger is the cause of physical violence and war. Greed is behind the wastage of natural resources and pollution of the environment, ultimately leading to starvation and poverty. Ignorance, which means being blind to the consequences of our actions, causes disease. It is imperative, therefore, to deal with these 'poisons' if we are to free ourselves from suffering.

As mentioned before, early Buddhist teachings sought to eradicate these 'poisons'. This is why many people have the impression that Buddhists live very austere lives. However, the eradication of instinctive behaviour ultimately denies life itself. Instinctive desires for food, sex and sleep are all necessary to preserve life. Indeed, desire is the driving force behind civilisation.

Desires are not always a source of suffering. They function in positive ways too: art is created through the desire to express beauty; science has developed in answer to hunger for knowledge. Eating, sleeping and sex are all very enjoyable activities as well as being necessary for survival. We therefore do not seek to get rid of desires, but rather transform them into enlightenment. Or, to put it the other way round, our deluded impulses are transformed by enlightenment.

This process is referred to in Nichiren Daishonin's Buddhism as *bonno soku bodai*. Deluded impulses (*bonno*) equal (*soku*) enlightenment (*bodai*). However, 'equal' is only an approximation of the true meaning of *soku*. *Soku* means that deluded impulses and Buddhahood are inseparable, that they both exist in everyone, and that the negative aspects of delusion can be transformed into enlightenment. In the same way, 'the sufferings of birth and death are transformed (*soku*) into nirvana'. We cannot achieve enlightenment outside of the reality of birth and death.

Fire is a good example of this transformation process. We use the logs of desire or suffering to build a fire of enlightened wisdom. Without the wood, light and heat cannot be generated. Wood is not the same as light, but through the cleansing and purifying action of fire, it becomes so. In a similar way, deluded impulses are transformed into enlightenment. This transformation process is *soku*. Nichiren Daishonin defined *soku* as Nam-myoho-renge-kyo.

Illusions, instinctive desires and negative impulses motivate us to take actions which cause us to suffer. This suffering, which we want to avoid, is the fuel which spurs us on to chant Nam-myoho-renge-kyo. This activates our Buddhahood from which arise such qualities as hope and courage, which allow us to deal with our suffering. At that moment, illusion is transformed into enlightenment, manifesting itself as wisdom, compassion and life-force.

Another way of looking at it is that human life, full of suffering, is shrouded in darkness, like being in a dark room. In order to see clearly, all that is required is to turn on the light. The room is the same place, whether dark or light. Similarly, our lives are essentially the same whether deluded or enlightened. Also, no matter how long the room has been dark, it still contains the potential to be light. However, we need a way to generate light and we can do it by chanting Nam-myoho-renge-kyo. Using this analogy, Nichiren Daishonin said:

> All the people of the ten worlds can attain Buddhahood. We can comprehend this when we remember that fire can be produced by a stone taken from the bottom of a river, and a candle can light up a place that has been dark for billions of years. If even the most ordinary things of this world are such wonders, then how much more wondrous is the power of the Mystic Law. [1]

When we chant Nam-myoho-renge-kyo, therefore, we do not deny desire. In fact, when starting to practise we are advised to chant for what we most want. This is because desire is such a great driving force that it makes our practice very strong. Also, our physical needs are important to our well-being. So if one's greatest desire is to get a job, that is naturally what will be at the forefront of one's mind whilst chanting. Through chanting, we generate hope and the wisdom to take the right action. The result is two-fold. Through this increase of wisdom and energy, we see a positive and tangible result: progress on the work front. However, the experience of the qualities of Buddhahood, welling up from within us, is far greater in the long term, than the tangible result.

Clearly our desires are many and varied. The ultimate aim of our practice is to realise Buddhahood and in so doing, achieve world peace. For many, it is natural to feel that world peace is their most cherished desire and to chant single-mindedly for this. Others are troubled by sickness in the family and focus their practice mainly on this. Some desires are more self-orientated, such as the desire for a mate or wanting to have a drink.

Whatever our desires may be, there is no need to feel guilty or to deny them. If we do this we are separating the idea of Buddhahood into some superhuman state of being, unattainable and removed from human life. Rather, we must use these desires as fuel to transform our lives and manifest enlightenment.

There are no rules in Nichiren Daishonin's Buddhism. Since we can reveal boundless wisdom through our practice, we can see any situation clearly and decide for ourselves what is the best way to act. If, for instance, we have a drink problem which causes ourselves and others to suffer, then we will gain the clarity to recognise this. Drinking is not wrong in itself. Only when the desire to drink controls our lives does it cause suffering. So we chant about our desires and gain the wisdom and determination necessary to put them in perspective.

Anything and everything which makes us a human being is potentially a great quality when transformed into Buddhahood. For example, someone who has a terrible temper can transform it into passion for world peace and a fulfilled life through chanting Nam-myoho-renge-kyo. As we continue to chant, the 'three poisons' of greed, anger and ignorance become the great qualities of the Buddha, known as the three properties: compassion, wisdom and life-force.

Fundamentally, our greatest desire is to grow as human beings, achieve clarity and live creatively. As Daisaku Ikeda says:

I believe in the existence of another kind of human desire: I call it the basic desire, and I believe that it is the force that actively propels all other human desires in the direction of creativity. It is the source of all impelling energy inherent in life; it is also the longing to unite one's life with the life of the universe and to draw vital energy from the universe. This basic desire transmits the pulsation of universal life to all human emotions and thus elevates their natures. Consequently, the various human desires generated by human life stimulate creativity while maintaining contact with the basic desire.[2]

1 *The Major Writings of Nichiren Daishonin*, Vol. 1, p. 223.
2 Arnold Toynbee & Daisaku Ikeda, *Choose Life: A Dialogue*, p. 332.

The
Oneness
of Body *and* Mind

'Life at each moment encompasses both
body and spirit'

‘What is matter? Never mind. What is mind? Never matter!’ For centuries, philosophers, theologians and scientists have argued about the nature of the basic components of life. Is life essentially composed entirely of matter, with mind and consciousness a by-product of the human brain? Or is it essentially spiritual, with the body merely a vessel? Or are mind and matter independent entities, which are in some way connected?

Generally speaking, there are two main schools of thought: those who see life in purely physical terms, and those who believe it is spiritual. This polarisation of viewpoints is demonstrated in the treatment of ill health. There is much evidence indicating the importance of a patient's positive attitude to recovery. Even so, the emphasis in medical science still lies heavily on physical treatments such as surgery and drugs. Conversely, faith healers often use treatments which are wholly spiritual.

It is widely accepted nowadays that the state of one's mind influences one's body, and equally that one's physical condition affects the state of one's mind. However, the practical implications of this inseparability remain largely in the realm of theory. On the whole, the separation between mind and body persists in science, medicine, religion and politics.

From the viewpoint of Nichiren Daishonin's Buddhism, body and mind are equal and interdependent. This principle is known as the oneness of body and mind (*shiki shin funi*). Body, or the material aspect (*shiki*), includes everything which can be outwardly discerned such as colour, form and texture. Mind, or spirit (*shin*), refers to those aspects of life which are inner or invisible such as emotions, will and personality.

Their oneness is indicated by the word *funi* which means 'two but not two' and 'not two but two'. This is not intended to be a riddle, but to clarify that although we can observe body and mind separately, in essence they are one. Neither is caused by the other. Furthermore, one cannot exist without the other. Both arise from the same fundamental entity: life itself.

A person can know another's mind by listening to his voice. This is because the physical aspect reveals the spiritual aspect. The physical and spiritual, which are one in essence, manifest themselves as two distinct aspects.[1]

All functions of life are revealed both physically and spiritually. Sleep refreshes the body, yet also has a vital psychological role. Reading a book, which inspires or entertains our minds, also involves the use of our bodies. Work, whether manual or desk-bound, involves both thought and physical exertion.

The unseen, spiritual workings of life are, of course, more difficult to analyse than visible actions. They can only be observed through their physical manifestations. Perhaps this is why the emphasis in the physical sciences has always been on matter. Yet when matter is reduced to its smallest particles, the difference between 'something' and 'nothing' becomes increasingly difficult to discern. Interestingly, recent scientific theories suggest that consciousness is inherent in life; all life, including objects such as stones. This idea comes closest to the Buddhist perception that all life, including insentient life, has both physical and spiritual aspects.

In society as a whole, we can see the shortcomings of placing emphasis on either the material or the spiritual. European societies have, in the past, placed spiritual values highly. Unfortunately, more often than not, this led to hypocrisy. For example, many people in power maintained their own physical comforts while placating those in poverty with the promise of rewards after death. However, certain minimum physical requirements are necessary to people's well-being. One cannot be said to be leading a fulfilled life if starving and cold. These dual standards, and the divorcing of the spiritual from the physical, tended to breed an attitude of resignation. In the second half of the twentieth century, the opportunity to achieve a good standard of living became available to many more people. Understandably, along with this, there arose a degree of scepticism as to the importance of spirituality and the value of religion in general.

Likewise, societies based on materialism, such as our own in the present day, demonstrate that it is virtually impossible to establish a truly prosperous society if no regard is paid to the spiritual self. It would seem that it is not possible for people to demonstrate integrity and overcome corruption if they have no personal spiritual values. People need values, such as honesty, even in the pursuit of materialism.

A constructive and fulfilling society must be based on the equal importance of both material and spiritual values. Since they are inseparable, there can be no mental well-being without physical well-being and vice-versa.

This is amply illustrated by the modern syndrome of stress. Stress can be caused by noise, hunger, death or financial anxiety, to name but a few environmental and psychological triggers. Equally, the effects of stress are both physical and mental, resulting in irritation, tension, depression, high blood pressure, stomach ulcers, irritable bowel syndrome and so on. Stress can be alleviated in many ways, such as positive thinking, exercise, even swimming with dolphins. It is becoming not just desirable, but vital, that in all fields of endeavour equal importance is given to the body and the mind.

In contrast to many other religions, the practice of Nichiren Daishonin's Buddhism is not directed solely towards spiritual enlightenment. It influences our lives at a fundamental level. Chanting Nam-myoho-renge-kyo affects us mentally in various ways, giving rise to optimism, determination and joy. At the same time, it affects every cell in our bodies. For this reason, posture and concentration are important when chanting, as well as a steady rhythm. Many people have found that chanting Nam-myoho-renge-kyo has helped them to overcome illness because it affects both body and mind.

Furthermore, our aim in practising Nichiren Daishonin's Buddhism is to improve all aspects of our lives. As well as developing ourselves spiritually, it is also important to fulfil ourselves at work and establish harmonious relationships. We therefore direct our chanting towards improvements in our material circumstances as well as towards our spiritual well-being.

Buddhism defines two kinds of benefit: conspicuous and inconspicuous. Conspicuous benefit corresponds to the body or material circumstances, while inconspicuous benefit corresponds to improvements in our character, such as increased wisdom and energy. At their root, these two kinds of benefit cannot be separated either. For example, increased wisdom leads us to take care of our health and discover what type of job suits us best; more energy is in itself healthy and enables us to be more active in society. Respect and compassion are also activated by our practice, naturally creating tolerance and harmony in our relationships with others. In discussing this subject Daisaku Ikeda says:

From ancient times, philosophers and theologians have formulated various concepts of the relationship between the mind and the body. The doctrines born of these concepts are numerous and different in kind, but all of them fall into one of two general categories: materialistic and spiritualistic. Followers of both ways have done much for the sake of cultural developments, and I believe that their achievements deserve proper evaluation. For example, by expounding morality and love, spiritualists have contributed greatly to keeping human society truly humane. For their part, the materialists have laid the foundations for the formation and development of modern science.

Still I am unable to embrace either approach without reservation. Although the materialists recognise man's spiritual functions, by considering the physical body the original source of being, they tend to view life itself as material in nature. Furthermore, while agreeing with the spiritualists that reason, intellect, desires and other mental functions are the bases of a truly humane way of life, I cannot subscribe to the philosophy that the physical aspects of human life and the physically related human desires are to be despised. Both the materialists and the spiritualists seem to pursue only one aspect of the issue and fail to grasp the relationship between spirit and body.[2]

1 *The Major Writings of Nichiren Daishonin*, Vol. 4, p. 32.
2 Arnold Toynbee & Daisaku Ikeda, *Choose Life: A Dialogue*, pp. 24-5.

The Oneness
of Self *and*
Environment

'There are not two lands, pure or impure in themselves. The difference lies solely in the good or evil of our minds.'

The destruction of our natural environment is of great concern, as the pollution of the land, sea and air increases at an alarming rate. Few people would deny that this has been caused by humankind's greed and selfishness. Social problems, too, are on the increase: homelessness, unemployment, drug abuse and the breakdown of the family, to name but a few.

According to Buddhism, the environment reflects the people who inhabit it. In his writings, Nichiren Daishonin says that life is like the body and the environment like a shadow. When the body bends, the shadow bends also.

We can see this relationship of body and shadow quite clearly in, for example, someone who is severely depressed. Such a person is likely to neglect his home and personal appearance. Others are mostly repelled by this, which reinforces that person's feeling of isolation, so the depression deepens. On the other hand, someone who is secure and generous creates a warm and attractive environment around them. Others are drawn to this and influenced by it, thereby widening the circle of warmth.

It is much harder to see this relationship in terms of ourselves. If we are, say, unhappy at work, we may think the problem lies with the company. However, according to Buddhism everything, including work, is the reflection of our inner lives. If we change ourselves, our circumstances will inevitably change also. Everything is perceived through the self and alters according to the individual's perception. Whether we enjoy our work or not has much more to do with our individual state of life than the situation itself.

Similarly, how we feel about the weather has much more to do with the state of our minds than whether the sky is blue or grey. Of course, the environment influences us as well, and most people feel better if it is a bright, sunny day. However, if we are feeling good inside, we can appreciate the wind and rain just as much as the sun.

The effect of the environment on people is seen, for example, in inner cities. Here, problems such as violence and vandalism are recognised as being influenced by urban environments where people live in densely populated areas. The effect human beings have on their environment is demonstrated by problems such as pollution. However, again, most of us regard pollution as being caused by someone else. Furthermore, most people consider it is up to the government or large business concerns to cure the problems, not only of pollution, but of all society's ills. This is not necessarily because we don't care, but because we often feel powerless to change our environment, viewing it as we do, as being created by other people.

The principle of the oneness of self and environment (*esho funi*) means that life (*sho*) and its environment (*e*) are inseparable (*funi*). *Funi* means 'two but not two'. This means that although we perceive things as separate from us, there is a dimension of our lives which is one with the universe. At the most fundamental level of life itself, there is no separation between ourselves and the environment. This fundamental level of life can be called the ultimate reality, defined by Nichiren Daishonin as Nam-myoho-renge-kyo.

The oneness of self and environment is further clarified by the doctrine of the three realms: the realm of the self, the realm of living beings and the realm of the environment. This classifies differences amongst individual living beings, their social and natural environments.

The realm of the self
In the realm of the self, each individual life consists of five components: form, perception, conception, volition and consciousness. Form is the physical aspect: male or female, tall or short, black or white etc. Form also includes the five sense organs - eyes, ears, tongue, nose and skin - through which we perceive the outer world.

THE THREE REALMS

THE REALM OF THE SELF	form, perception, conception, volition and consciousness
THE REALM OF LIVING BEINGS	society
THE REALM OF THE LAND	the natural environment

The other four components are mental aspects of individual life. Perception is the function of receiving information through the senses. This varies depending on both the quality of the information received and the awareness of the individual. Conception is the function of analysing the received information and forming a coherent mental picture of it. Volition is the will to take action based on this information. Consciousness, which includes judgement and wisdom, is the integrating function which unifies these thought processes.

The five components are common to everyone, but no two individuals are exactly alike. Our special characteristics and personality are expressed through the five components. These are constantly changing. Our bodies change as we get older and most of our cells are replaced every seven years. Our thoughts are also constantly changing. The realm of the self is therefore a temporary combination of the five components.

In his writings, Nichiren Daishonin explains the far-reaching implications of this realm of the self:

> Therefore, when the people's five sense organs are disordered, the four quarters [of the earth] as well as the centre will be startled and shaken, and as signs of the consequent destruction of the land, mountains will collapse, grasses and trees wither and rivers run dry.[1]

This is an incredible statement, even today. However, we can see the reality of environmental destruction caused by humankind before our very eyes.

The realm of living beings

Each individual is born into a social environment: the realm of living beings. This category accounts for cultural and hereditary differences between social groups. A person is a product of his social environment, and equally contributes to and modifies his cultural or family group. The realm of society closely reflects the lives of the people living in it.

The realm of living beings also pertains to other creatures. We tend to think that there is one large environment in which all life dwells. However, when we look more closely we see that each living being, as well as each social group, inhabits a unique environment. For instance, we don't come across whales living in trees. Likewise, as yet, no human being is living at the bottom of the ocean (if he did so he would have to create a special environment). Within a single footstep, in fact, there are a myriad different habitats occupied by insect life and micro-organisms. Each species inhabits the most suitable environment and adapts to it. Equally, each species modifies that environment to suit its own requirements.

The realm of the natural environment

The third realm, that of the land, is where living beings dwell in their social groups. For thousands of years, human beings have seen the environment as separate and even hostile. We have sought to dominate and exploit the land, largely ignorant of our delicate symbiotic relationship with it. As a result, far from constructing the perfect environment we sought to create, we have all but destroyed the habitat on which our life depends.

Many people are exerting tremendous efforts to reverse this trend, and are creating a widespread awareness of the problems.

The United Nations World Council on Environment and Development has called for sustainable development based on harmony between environmental protection and economic development. To achieve this, international cooperation and agreement is required. It also involves different fields of endeavour, such as science, economy, commerce, agriculture and manufacturing.

The situation is extremely serious and the efforts of concerned people who are actively involved in trying to remedy it, whether globally or locally, are of vital importance. If we truly understand the oneness of self and environment, we can see that everything depends on each one of us. As stated in the slogan of the 1992 UN Conference for Environmental Development: 'Think Globally, Act Locally'.

From the Buddhist perspective, the only lasting way to bring about change is for people themselves to change. As the above quotation says, 'There are not two lands, pure or impure in themselves. The difference lies solely in the good or evil of our minds.'[2] 'Evil' means self-centred and short-term actions based on greed, arrogance, fear and aggression.

Nichiren Daishonin teaches us that we possess Buddhahood, the enlightened life-condition of the human being, and can therefore transform our negative tendencies into creative and valuable ones. The single most positive action we can make for society and the land is to transform our own lives, so that they are no longer dominated by anger, greed and fear. When we manifest wisdom, generosity and integrity, we naturally make more valuable choices. We call this transformation of the self 'human revolution'. Hence, the foreword to the novel entitled *The Human Revolution* says:

A great revolution of character in just a single individual will help achieve a change in the destiny of a nation and further, will cause a change in the destiny of all humankind.[3]

Most of all, it is lack of respect for ourselves and our environment which causes the problems we are facing today. Often, we cannot foresee the long-term results of our actions. However, if we base our decisions on the utmost respect for all life, our actions will be wiser. The principle of the oneness of self and environment explains that everything is interconnected. Short-term profit, if detrimental to the environment, therefore rebounds on us, both individually and collectively. In the same way, actions which contribute to the well-being of other living beings and the environment will also benefit our own lives.

We are free to choose the path we follow, and the ability to follow the right one is innate within man. The question is how to develop the potential wisdom inherent in our life-force so that it works for life and creativity in the universe. Even if a human being possesses the ability to love and trust, if the motivating force within him is weak, he is not apt to influence other human beings, let alone human life as a whole. On the other hand, if a person has a strong motivating force, but is beset by doubt, suspicion and antagonism towards others, he is apt to destroy himself, and perhaps humankind as a whole. When we have discovered how to employ our life-force for the creation and furtherance of life on both the human and the cosmic levels, and when we have found out how to live in true harmony with the universe, the philosophy of the unity between subjective existence and objective environment will have become the great saving practical philosophy of humankind.[4]

1 *The Major Writings of Nichiren Daishonin*, Vol. 4, p. 146.
2 *Major Writings*, Vol. 1, p. 4.
3 Daisaku Ikeda, *The Human Revolution*, (1961) Vol. 1, p. iii.
4 Daisaku Ikeda, *Life, An Enigma, A Precious Jewel*, p. 45.

The
Middle Way

'Life is indeed an elusive reality that
transcends both the words and concepts
of existence and non-existence. It is
neither existence nor non-existence, yet
exhibits the qualities of both. It is the
mystic entity of the Middle Way that is the
reality of all things.'

The sole purpose of Buddhist philosophy is for people to overcome suffering and establish true happiness. The early Buddhist sutras taught that suffering was the result of trying to cling on to people and things, which by their very nature are temporary. We die, loved ones die, fortunes change. Life is in a continual state of flux. In the early days of Buddhism, therefore, people devoted themselves to eliminating their attachments to temporary things through various meditations and practices.

However, trying to detach oneself is, in the end, not an answer. Getting rid of all attachments includes ridding oneself of the desire to eat, sleep, have sex and so on. This extreme approach ultimately leads to a denial of life itself. This cannot be said to be the secret to a happy life!

In order to clarify the true nature of life, Mahayana Buddhists formulated the concept of the middle way. Although a familiar sounding phrase, its meaning in Buddhism has nothing to do with compromise. While it may seem, at first glance, to be advocating 'moderation in all things', it goes well beyond that idea. It does not mean to steer a middle course between extremes; rather, it means to unify and transcend duality.

The middle way derives from a principle, central to Buddhist philosophy, known as the unification of the three truths. These are the truth of non-substantiality (*ku*), the truth of temporary existence (*ke*), and the truth of the middle way (*chu*). Although all life can be viewed from these three aspects, they cannot be separated, so they are sometimes called the threefold truth.

The truth of non-substantiality (*ku*) means that nothing in life is unchanging or fixed. The nature of all things is *ku*, or potentiality, which cannot be defined as either existence or non-existence. The concept of *ku* is often understood to mean nothingness, void or emptiness, but this is not at all its true meaning. On the contrary, *ku* indicates the infinite potential of life at each and every moment.

The truth of temporary existence (*ke*) means that whilst all things are non-substantial, they do have a temporary existence. The truth of the middle way (*chu*) is that everything is both non-substantiality and temporary existence, yet its essence is neither of these. *Chu* is the true entity of life, defined by Nichiren Daishonin as Nam-myoho-renge-kyo.

All of this is rather hard to grasp. Indeed, the true entity (*chu*) is beyond the limitation of words or concepts. But if we consider some examples, we can get an idea of what it means. If we look at a chestnut tree, we see that it changes from season to season, dropping its leaves in winter, flowering in spring and producing nuts in autumn. The way the tree changes each season, the life-span of the tree and its health, all correspond to the truth of non-substantiality (*ku*). Its outward physical appearance, at each stage of its cycle, corresponds to the truth of temporary existence (*ke*). The tree itself is *chu*. It is at the same time unified with nature and unique in itself, possessing the capacity to produce nuts instead of, say, apples.

All things can be seen in terms of these three truths, including inanimate objects. If we take the example of a mirror, it has the potential to be clear, dirty, chipped and so on, which corresponds to the truth of non-substantiality. Any images it reflects are its physical aspect, or the truth of temporary existence. The mirror itself is the entity, or the middle way.

In terms of human beings, we can see the truth of temporary existence (*ke*) in the way a person looks and speaks which corresponds to the physical self. The truth of non-substantiality (*ku*) refers to the mind or spirit, which has unlimited potential. The truth of the middle way (*chu*), or the entity of a person's life, is the inherent capacity to be unique as well as at one with the universe. This entity is often called the true self, the greater self, or the universal self. Between birth and old age a person changes many times, both physically and mentally. Nevertheless, there is always something about an individual which is intrinsically the same. This

THE THREE TRUTHS

KE	the truth of temporary existence
KU	the truth of non-substantiality
CHU	the truth of the middle way

is the entity of life: it is what makes each person unique, what makes us human, and what connects us to the universe.

If we have difficulty grasping this concept it is because we are trying to separate the three truths. This is not the intention of the analysis. It is quite the reverse. The Japanese term for the three truths is *santai* which means three (*san*) and to be obvious or clear (*tai*). Obviously, or clearly, we can look at life from any of these three viewpoints but, since each one contains the other three and they are unified, we cannot separate them.

There are many ways in which dualistic thinking has underlain the development of our civilisation: the separation of mind and body; the separation of man and nature; the separation of good and evil. This has led to many problems in society. The oneness of mind and body, and of self and environment, are discussed elsewhere in this book, so let us consider good and evil.

Traditional folklore is about 'goodies' and 'baddies'. There are, for example, very few European fairy stories where the 'baddies' turn into 'goodies'. Buddhist literature, however, is full of fables in which demons turn into gods. This is because Buddhism views people as neither good nor bad intrinsically. Rather, at each moment we have the potential to exhibit either enlightenment or delusion.

From the viewpoint of the unification of the three truths, when we are deluded, the physical aspect of our lives (*ke*) manifests itself as greed. Greed is the insatiable desire to fulfil our own physical needs, regardless of the needs of others. Our mental aspect (*ku*) manifests itself as anger - the desire to dominate others and to be right at all times. The entity of our lives (*chu*), when deluded is, as it were, shrouded in fundamental darkness, blind to the true nature of life. This is usually called ignorance or stupidity. It is the fundamental illusion from which both greed and anger arise.

When enlightened, the physical aspect of our lives is transformed into compassion: empathy for others and a desire to help them overcome their suffering. The mental aspect is transformed into wisdom: the capacity to see the best course of action in order to improve the quality of life for everyone and everything. The essential aspect of life, or the middle way, becomes the source of life-force itself, which is unified with the life-force of the cosmos. From this fundamental enlightened life, or the greater self, compassion and wisdom are able to flow freely.

However, we need a way to access this greater self, or universal energy. Nichiren Daishonin taught us how to do so:

A mind which presently is clouded by illusions originating from the innate darkness of life is like a tarnished mirror, but once it is polished it will become clear, reflecting the enlightenment of immutable truth. Arouse deep faith and polish your mirror night and day. How should you polish it? Only by chanting Nam-myoho-renge-kyo.[1]

Chanting Nam-myoho-renge-kyo enables us to return our lives to the source of fundamental life-force, or the greater self, and live with wisdom and compassion, without denying any aspect of our lives. We can then fully appreciate everything life has to offer. This is the middle way which unifies and overcomes the contradictions of a 'lesser self' based solely on the limited and changeable physical and mental aspects of life.

We can see the importance of the approach of the middle way in society. The mental aspect of life (*ku*), where ideas are formed, is the driving force behind the progress of civilisation. The physical aspect of life (*ke*) works to create harmony in ourselves, with others and with nature. The middle way (*chu*) is the unchanging foundation of life itself, which supports and stabilises the other two.

All three aspects are needed for a healthy society. Progress without harmony leads to idealism. Ideas only become practical and worthwhile when placed in the context of the needs of others and the laws of nature. On the other hand, if every great idea was scrapped because it was considered to be too difficult, then progress would be sacrificed for the sake of harmony and this would lead to stagnation. Harmony without a firm foundation leads to apathy or compromise. Progress without a creative basis becomes destructive. All three aspects - harmony, progress and life-force - are needed for the betterment of society. This is what is meant by the middle way.

To live for the greater self does not mean abandoning the lesser self. The lesser self is only able to act because of the existence of the greater self. Desires and attachments experienced by all of us as smaller selves have stimulated the advance of civilisation. If man had not been attracted to wealth, economic growth could not have taken place. If man had not struggled to overcome the natural elements and provide relief from such things as cold, the natural sciences would not have flourished. Without the mutual attachment and conflict of the sexes, literature would have been deprived of one of its most famous and enduring fields of expression... Desire and all it implies constitute a generative moving force in life. But they and the smaller self they affect most directly must be correctly orientated. Buddhist teaching strives to discover the greater self and, instead of suppressing or eliminating the smaller self, to control and direct it so that it can contribute to the growth of a better world civilisation through its relation with the greater self.[2]

1 *The Major Writings of Nichiren Daishonin*, Vol. 1, p. 5.
2 Daisaku Ikeda, *A Lasting Peace*, Vol. 1, pp. 122-3.

The
True Entity
of All Phenomena

'Life at each moment encompasses both body and spirit and both self and environment of all sentient beings, in every condition of life, as well as insentient beings - plants, sky and earth, on down to the most minute particles of dust. Life at each moment permeates the universe and is revealed in all phenomena. One awakened to this truth himself embodies this relationship.'

Ever since we human beings became conscious of our existence on this planet, we have asked ourselves such questions as 'Why are we here?' 'How can we make sense of our existence in this world?' 'What is life all about?' During the last century, physicists and mathematicians have been searching for one law which encompasses all laws, what is referred to as the 'theory of everything'. They have yet to find an answer.

The search for answers to these questions has also, naturally, been the pursuit of Buddhist scholars. In observing the nature of life, one sees constant change. However, life also manifests an overall consistency. What is the law which unifies and encompasses this constant state of flux? In Buddhism this is referred to as the true entity of all phenomena. The word entity is used here to mean all-encompassing wholeness - that which embraces all the seemingly separate parts.

The Lotus Sutra refers to the true entity of all phenomena like this:

> The true entity of all phenomena can only be understood and shared between Buddhas. This reality consists of the appearance, nature, entity, power, influence, inherent cause, relation, latent effect, manifest effect, and their consistency from beginning to end.[1]

This list of the different modes of reality is called the ten factors. These ten factors, or aspects of life, are common to all beings. They are: (1) appearance, or form - the physical aspect of life; (2) nature - mind, spirit, and character; (3) entity - life itself. This factor unites the first two. These first three factors signify the physical and spiritual reality of life (also see p.59).

The following six factors describe the way in which life operates: (4) power - inherent energy; (5) influence - the effect of one's power on the outer world; (6) inherent cause - our inner tendency to react in habitual ways; (7) relation, or external cause - an external cause acts as a stimulus with which we interact. The combination of inherent cause and relation triggers two effects: (8) latent effect - an unseen effect lodged in the depths of one's life, and (9) manifest effect - the actual appearance of latent effects. Factors six to nine describe the way in which we change from moment to moment and define the mechanics of karma (also see p.31). (10) Consistency from beginning to end - this means that all the factors are consistent with one another.

To see how the four factors of cause and effect work, let us consider the example of a thief. The inherent cause for his stealing might be excessive greed. This is activated when he sees an open window and money on a table - relation. He reaches inside to take the money. He appears to get away with it, but does he? He has engraved further in his life the tendency, or latent effect, of greed and dishonesty. The manifest effect - of being stolen from himself, for instance, or being caught and locked up in jail - may take time to appear, but it definitely will appear at some time, perhaps even in a future lifetime.

Like the saying, 'Once a thief, always a thief', the tenth factor, consistency from beginning to end, means that he will always be at the mercy of his greed, unless he makes a dedicated effort to change his karma. Consistency from beginning to end also means that all factors are consistent with each other at any given time. The thief's physical appearance will betray deviousness to others. His mind will be cunning, his life will be self-centred. His power and influence will be detrimental to society. His causes and effects will be consistent with his greedy nature. Of course, at other times, for instance when at home with his family, his ten factors could be expressed quite differently as he demonstrates his love and affection.

Life is constantly changing. The theory of the ten factors shows how it changes. It is not easy to grasp because of all ten factors, only physical appearance and manifest effect are visible. The others are unseen, or sometimes both seen and unseen. For instance, in the case of the money on the table, the money is visible but the relationship the thief has with it is not.

To see how the ten factors explain change, let's consider another example. A young man is walking along the street listening to his Walkman. He could be in rapture listening to the sound of his favourite music. His mind would be completely immersed in this. His physical appearance would be inward-looking, perhaps totally oblivious to those around. His power and influence would be very limited at that moment, since he would be in a world of his own. Suppose someone laid a hand on his arm to stop him and ask for directions. This would be an external cause, or relation. His reaction changes his state of life. He may lash out, thinking he is being attacked, showing both fear and anger ingrained deeply in his life (inherent cause). But instead, he takes his earphones off, smiles and patiently explains the directions - he's a nice guy (tranquillity as inherent cause). This has its effects, latent and manifest. He gets a nice smile and thank you (manifest effect), he feels good inside (latent effect). All of his other factors change at that moment, as observed in his physical appearance, which would be open and animated.

The ten factors are part of a total theory of the mechanics of life, termed 'three thousand realms in a momentary existence of life' (*ichinen sanzen*). The figure three thousand is arrived at by multiplying the ten states, the three realms and the ten factors (see chart p.68). Each of the ten states contains within itself the potential to express all ten states, making one hundred life-conditions. These are expressed in all three realms, thus giving three hundred conditions. The ten factors of life make the total up to three thousand realms in each moment of existence.

The sixth century Chinese Buddhist scholar, T'ien-t'ai, established the doctrine of 'three thousand realms in a

THREE THOUSAND REALMS IN A MOMENTARY EXISTENCE OF LIFE

TEN STATES OF LIFE

BUDDHAHOOD	enlightenment
BODHISATTVA	caring for others
ABSORPTION	realisation
LEARNING	self-reflection
RAPTURE	heaven
TRANQUILLITY	humanity
ANGER	self-righteousness
ANIMALITY	instinctive behaviour
HUNGER	greed
HELL	extreme suffering

TEN FACTORS

1	APPEARANCE	physical aspect
2	NATURE	mental aspect
3	ENTITY	substance, life itself
4	POWER	inherent energy
5	INFLUENCE	influence of power
6	INHERENT CAUSE	habit or karma
7	RELATION	external cause
8	LATENT EFFECT	potential effect
9	MANIFEST EFFECT	visible outcome
10	CONSISTENCY FROM BEGINNING TO END	

THREE REALMS

THE REALM OF THE SELF	form, perception, conception, volition and consciousness
THE REALM OF LIVING BEINGS	society
THE REALM OF THE LAND	the natural environment

momentary existence of life', based on an exhaustive study of the Lotus Sutra. This theory explains how life, at each moment, changes in many different ways, while at the same time maintaining an overall consistency. This means that each individual life permeates the universe in three thousand ways and that three thousand changing aspects of the universe are contained in each individual. His analysis clarified the true entity of all phenomena taught in the Lotus Sutra.

The figure three thousand is not intended to be used as a mathematical formula. Rather, it indicates the many complex and dynamic ways in which life interacts. It signifies that the experience of life (and death) is common to all things, including insentient life. Most importantly, there is no fundamental difference between a Buddha and an ordinary person.

When Shakyamuni first taught the ten factors in the 'Expedient Means' chapter of the Lotus Sutra, it was revolutionary. Prior to this, it was thought that people were stuck in the same life-state, such as hell or anger, at least for the present lifetime. The ten factors mean, in essence, that everyone can attain Buddhahood, because everyone, Buddha and common mortal alike, possesses these ten factors. The ultimate goal of our Buddhist practice is to establish Buddhahood as our basic life-tendency, thereby transforming ourselves and our environment.

Shakyamuni taught the Lotus Sutra in a subjective way, that is he taught through his enlightened experience of life. T'ien-t'ai, in the doctrine of the 'three thousand realms in a momentary existence of life', taught by more abstract, philosophical means. He advocated meditation on this 'region of the unfathomable' in order to arrive at an enlightened life-condition. In practice, the number of people who could achieve this was extremely limited.

Nichiren Daishonin, in thirteenth century Japan, wanted all

people to be enlightened to the true entity of all phenomena. He is called the Buddha of the True Cause because he revealed the true entity of all phenomena to be Myoho-renge-kyo. He explained that the fundamental cause for attaining enlightenment is chanting Nam-myoho-renge-kyo. Furthermore, he crystallised the doctrine of 'three thousand realms in a momentary existence of life' in the Gohonzon, thereby giving us a graphic representation of the true entity of all phenomena (see p.85). By chanting Nam-myoho-renge-kyo to the Gohonzon every day, we draw forth and strengthen our Buddha state, dispensing with the need for difficult meditation or ways of life which are removed from society.

The Lotus Sutra says that the true entity of all phenomena can only be understood and shared between Buddhas. This is because, ultimately, we have to experience it in order to understand it. Many people tend to think that the true entity, or law, exists in an abstract form which governs phenomena, a form such as a god. However, Buddhism teaches that the true entity does not exist apart from phenomena. All phenomena are themselves the true entity, seen from an enlightened life-condition. When we put Nichiren Daishonin's teachings into practice, we experience the theory of 'three thousand realms in a momentary existence of life' as a reality. We experience our lives permeating the universe, and the universe being contained within us. This harmony and integration influences our environment limitlessly.

Daisaku Ikeda has underlined the importance of answering the fundamental questions of life:

In order for human beings to live lives worthy of their humanity, they must return to a cognisance of their nature as part of the universal life-force and must regard this as the basis of all their actions. Once they have adopted this attitude, they will be able to create the sense of value that is urgently needed today. This sense of value will give paramount place to life itself, and it will devote major concern to solving the questions involved with life, for these are the ones that determine the answers to all other questions.[2]

---

1 *The Lotus Sutra* trans. Burton Watson, p. 24.
2 Arnold Toynbee & Daisaku Ikeda, *Choose Life, A Dialogue*, p. 139.

The
Eternity *of* Life

'If you wish to free yourself from the sufferings of birth and death you have endured through eternity and attain supreme enlightenment in this lifetime, you must awaken to the mystic truth which has always been within your life. This truth is Myoho-renge-kyo.'

The Buddhist view of the eternity of life is expressed as follows:
If when wide awake we examine our true nature, we will find no beginning that requires our being born and no end that requires our dying.[1]

It is certainly true that if we look back, we cannot remember a beginning to our lives. Our subjective experience of life is that it has always existed and always will exist. Apart from our feelings, of course, there is no proof whatsoever as to what will happen when we die. Belief in the eternity of life lies in the realm of faith.

Nevertheless, there are things we observe about the nature of life which lend support to the idea that life continues. For example, the rhythm of nature is cyclic. Although most plants appear lifeless in the winter, they grow again in the spring. In fact, everything we observe in nature goes through cycles. It is we human beings who have invented the notion of a straight line with a beginning and an end. We also know from science that matter cannot be destroyed, but rather changes into another form of energy. When, for instance, we burn something it is not destroyed, but changes into gases and residual matter.

Both our own experience and the observation of natural cycles make it logical to suppose that life continues in some way, rather than coming to an abrupt stop. In accordance with this, Buddhism explains the continuous cycle of life and death throughout eternity.

Myoho, of Nam-myoho-renge-kyo, means life and death. *Myoho* is usually translated as Mystic Law. This law encompasses the two aspects of life and death. It is called mystic because it is difficult to comprehend. *Myoho* also means seen and unseen, or latent and manifest.

We experience these phases of life and death all the time. For example, one minute we are happy and the next, angry. Where did the happiness go? We cannot say it does not exist, because it will appear again when the circumstances are right. Likewise, we cannot say it exists, because it is not here at this moment, yet we know it has not gone forever. This is the nature of everything - it comes and goes, at one moment manifest and at the next, latent. This state of neither existence nor non-existence is called *ku* (also see p.59).

The rain cycle is a good illustration of the phases of life and death. Rain falls and is absorbed into the earth. It reappears in streams and rivers, eventually flowing to the ocean. When the water evaporates, it loses its visible form temporarily, until it condenses into clouds and becomes rain again. Even though we cannot see the water vapour, we know it is still there, in its invisible form of H_2O. The visible water is like life, and the unseen water vapour like death. The water vapour has the potential (*ku*) to become rain when the circumstances are right. This continues in a never-ending cycle, which is why it makes such a good analogy for the cycle of life and death.

The life-death cycle is often compared to alternate periods of being awake and asleep. Sleep refreshes us, physically and mentally. Likewise, death is necessary to restore our energy in preparation for a new life. How, then, does Buddhism explain death and rebirth? Our lives have three aspects: body, mind and entity (also see p.59). At the time of death, all three aspects merge with the universe, passing from a sentient to an insentient state. An individual life becomes indistinguishable from universal life. Nichiren Daishonin explains:

> The Buddha, perfectly enlightened in the Three Bodies [body, mind and entity], takes the entire universe as his true body, takes the entire universe as his spiritual nature, takes the entire universe as his physical existence.[2]

At the time of death, all three aspects of our lives become one with the eternal flow of the universe. The individual workings of the physical and mental aspects of life are no longer distinguishable from the whole. This is quite different from the idea of transmigration of the 'soul' which is found in other religions. Buddhism denies the existence of soul. The individual entity does not go to some particular place like heaven, nor does it 'wander about' in an unseen form. It is united with the universe.

This can be compared to an iceberg melting into the ocean. While it exists, an iceberg has a massive unseen portion under the surface of the water. Likewise, individuals have huge potential, most of which is not apparent. When we die all of this, seen and unseen, melts back into universal life. The entity of an individual life continues in the state of *ku*, which transcends existence and non-existence. When the circumstances are appropriate, the individual manifestation of the entity will be born. This continues in a never-ending process, just like the rain cycle.

How rebirth happens is beyond everyday comprehension. Similarly, we do not know what happens while we are asleep. Where does our conscious mind go? While we are asleep it seems to vanish, yet when we wake up it returns. This is explained by the concept of *ku*. According to Buddhism, this is the state we enter when we die.

There are many things about life which are sources of wonder. For instance, a single cell has the inbuilt capacity to produce a fully grown and integrated human being. This is almost beyond imagination, yet happens as a common, everyday occurrence. Similarly, life and death defy ordinary descriptions of space and time.

Life cannot be consumed by the fire at the end of the kalpa, nor can it be washed away by floods. It can be neither cut by swords nor pierced by arrows. Although it can fit inside a mustard seed, the seed does not expand, nor does life contract. Although it fills the vastness of space, space is not too wide, nor is life too small.[3]

This poetic description of the nature of life opens our minds to a concept which is beyond time and space. We tend to think that our lives are confined within our skins. Yet when we are at work, our influence is still present at home. We are part of our friends' lives even if they are thousands of miles away. Our lives are not confined just to the space occupied by our physical bodies. Furthermore, whether we think about it or not, our lives are integrated with the universe as a whole. We are, at the same time, individual and universal. Viewed like this, it becomes conceivable that when we are in the phase of death, we are merged with the universe and yet retain the seeds of our individuality.

An individual life in the state of *ku* is not necessarily at peace, just as sleep is not always restful. While alive, we have the power to change our life-condition from moment to moment in response to external influences. If we feel sad, a friend coming round can cheer us up. However, while in *ku*, one has no power to change one's life-condition.

At the approach of death, external influences like money and power fade into insignificance. A person whose life was dominated by greed may become tortured by frustration. Someone who spent his life seeking power may become terrified. A person who has lived a wise and fulfilled life may feel contented and look forward to his next life, satisfied with his achievements in this one.

Our dominant state of life remains fixed in death and we are reborn into that same life-state (see ten states, p.21). We are born into circumstances which are exactly right for us. So, from the Buddhist point of view, conception involves not only the sexual union of the parents, but also the entity of life of the potential child.

It may be misleading to give specific examples, as life is complex. However, for the sake of clarification, suppose someone was extremely selfish and misused other people's love for these selfish ends. This would be making the cause to be unloved in the future. Hence, this person may be reborn to parents who are undemonstrative and never cuddle their child. In later life, the person might think it was the parents' fault that he or she is unable to develop a loving relationship. However, in the light of Buddhism, it was the child who determined this outcome as an effect of causes made in a past life. To put it another way, these circumstances offer the opportunity to change this selfish tendency. This is not to make a moral judgment, but to acknowledge that selfishness is small-minded and makes us unhappy. A large part of happiness is to be able to give freely to others. Of course, tensions in child/parent relationships are also determined by the life-condition of the parents. So, the right circumstances for birth depend on parents and child as well as environment.

There are innumerable different circumstances for birth: rich or poor; man or woman; race and culture. Individual karma accounts for these. While alive, we have the opportunity to shape our own future through the causes we make. If we believe that life is eternal and that the effects of these causes continue, there is all the more reason to challenge our weaknesses in this lifetime.

Belief in the eternity of life gives us perspective and security. Fear of all kinds stems ultimately from fear of death. When we experience the oneness of life and death, the oneness of ourselves and the universe, we feel calm and happy. Life becomes a source of wonder and joy. There is no longer any need to cling on to people and possessions. From the viewpoint of eternity, this life is but a fleeting moment. From another point of view, the present moment is itself eternity. Expressing our true humanity and savouring each moment is real happiness.

Cycles of life and death can be likened to the alternating periods of sleeping and wakefulness. We can understand death as a state in which, just as sleep prepares us for the next day's activities, we rest and replenish ourselves for a new life. Viewed in this light, death is not to be reviled, but should be acknowledged with life, as a blessing to be appreciated. The Lotus Sutra, the core of Mahayana Buddhism, states that the purpose of existence - the eternal cycles of life and death - is to be 'happy and at ease'. It further teaches that sustained faith and practice enable us to know a deep and abiding joy in death as well as life, to be equally 'happy and at ease' with both. Nichiren Daishonin describes the attainment of this state as the 'greatest of all joys'.

If the tragedies of this century of war and revolution have taught us anything, it is the folly of viewing the reform of external factors, such as social systems, as the sole determinant of human happiness. I am convinced that in the coming century, foremost importance must and will be placed on an inward-directed reformation, inspired by a new understanding of life and death.[4]

1 *Nichiren Daishonin Gosho Zenshu* (Japanese Collected Writings), p. 563.
2 *Gosho Zenshu*, p. 562.
3 *Gosho Zenshu*, p. 563.
4 Daisaku Ikeda, *A New Humanism*, p. 153.

The **Meaning** *of* **Nam-myoho-renge-kyo**

'This truth is *Myoho-renge-kyo. Chanting Myoho-renge-kyo will therefore enable you to grasp the mystic truth within you. Myoho-renge-kyo is the king of sutras, flawless in both letter and principle.*'

Nichiren Daishonin first declared Nam-myoho-renge-kyo on 28 April 1253. He had entered the priesthood at the age of fifteen, with the devoted aim of finding the ultimate teaching of Buddhism. He attained enlightenment through his own efforts and continued his studies so that he could find a way of making this wonderful state of life available to everyone.

After sixteen years of studying the sutras, Nichiren Daishonin declared that the Lotus Sutra contains the ultimate Buddhist teaching: namely, that everyone without exception has the potential to be a Buddha and that life is eternal. Further, the essence of these teachings is contained within the sutra's title. As he says in one of his letters:

> Included within the word Japan is all that is within the country's sixty-six provinces: all of the people and animals, the rice paddies and other fields, those of high and low status, the nobles and the commoners, the seven kinds of gems and all other treasures. Similarly, included within the title, Nam-myoho-renge-kyo, is the entire sutra consisting of all eight volumes, twenty-eight chapters and 69,384 characters without exception... Everything has its essential point and the heart of the Lotus Sutra is its title, Nam-myoho-renge-kyo.[1]

The title of the Lotus Sutra in Chinese characters is Myoho-renge-kyo. Chinese characters are pictorial; they encapsulate the essence of a concept, making this the most suitable language for the concise expression of profound principles. The word *nam* derives from Sanskrit and means 'to devote'. Literally, Nam-myoho-renge-kyo could be translated as 'Devotion to the Sutra of the Lotus Blossom of the Wonderful Law'.

To Nichiren Daishonin, Myoho-renge-kyo was far more than the title of a Buddhist text. It is the expression of the ultimate truth to which he was enlightened. It is the true entity of all phenomena, the Buddha nature inherent in all life, sentient and insentient. Chanting Nam-myoho-renge-kyo enables us to fuse our lives with the ultimate law and immediately manifest enlightenment.

Myoho

Myoho means Mystic Law. It is called mystic (*myo*) because it is difficult to discern. *Ho* means all phenomena. *Myoho* means that all phenomena and the ultimate law are one. As stated in 'On Attaining Buddhahood':

What then does *myo* signify? It is simply the mysterious nature of our lives from moment to moment, which the mind cannot comprehend nor words express. When you look into your own mind at any moment, you perceive neither colour nor form to verify that it exists. Yet you still cannot say it does not exist, for many differing thoughts continually occur to you. Life is indeed an elusive reality that transcends both the words and concepts of existence and non-existence. It is neither existence nor non-existence, yet exhibits the qualities of both. It is the mystic entity of the middle way that is the reality of all things. *Myo* is the name given to the mystic nature of life, and *ho* to its manifestations.[2]

The word mystic, then, has nothing to do with other-wordly experiences. Rather, an enlightened person is able to perceive the oneness of the ultimate reality (*myo*) and everyday life (*ho*). If we live based only on *ho* - all phenomena, or changing circumstances - we are confused and deluded. Enlightenment is signified by *myo* - the perception of the true nature of universal life. However, *myo* and *ho* are inseparable. This oneness is what is meant by the middle way. There is no fundamental distinction between enlightenment (*myo*) and delusion (*ho*), it just depends on whether we are seeing the whole picture.

In the same vein, *myoho* also means life (*ho*) and death (*myo*); seen (*ho*) and unseen (*myo*); manifest (*ho*) and latent (*myo*). These aspects of life are two phases of the universal law. We have difficulty grasping the whole picture because of the unseen, latent phase.

Myo has three more meanings: to open, to be endowed and perfect, and to revive. Opening refers to the energy, inherent in the universe, to create life. It also means the potential to open up one's life to reveal Buddhahood, thereby overcoming illusion. To be endowed and perfect means that every element of life contains the whole within itself; *myo* contains all truths and encompasses all phenomena. To revive refers to the regenerative force of nature. It also indicates that anyone, however deluded, has the capacity to awaken to their Buddha nature.

It is possible to see from this short explanation that the meanings of *myoho* expand ever outwards to encompass all laws and all phenomena. This is also the case for the other characters in Nam-myoho-renge-kyo. Ultimately, this phrase contains all Buddhist philosophy.

Renge

Renge literally means lotus flower. It indicates the simultaneity of cause and effect. This is because the lotus produces seeds and flowers at the same time. The lotus was also traditionally respected throughout the east for its auspicious qualities. It appeared frequently in paintings and literature, indicating purity, longevity and fertility as well as beauty.

In the same way as Myoho-renge-kyo goes far beyond just a title, *renge* goes far beyond being the name of a flower. It is the law of the simultaneity of cause and effect. Nichiren Daishonin said:

> The supreme principle was originally without a name. When the sage was observing the principle and assigning names to all things, he perceived that there is this wonderful single law (*myoho*) which simultaneously possesses both cause and effect (*renge*), and he named it *myoho-renge*. This single law that is *myoho-renge* encompasses within it all the phenomena comprising the ten states and the three thousand realms, and is lacking in none of them. Anyone who practises this law will obtain both the cause and the effect of Buddhahood simultaneously.[3]

This means that when we chant Nam-myoho-renge-kyo (cause) the state of Buddhahood (effect) immediately wells up from within us. This simultaneity of cause and effect is very important. In earlier forms of Buddhism, the effects of various practices were thought to emerge much later, even in a future lifetime. Perhaps because of these earlier Buddhist teachings, people tend to think that the law of cause and effect, karma, is fatalistic (also see p.31). However, the way in which our individual karma manifests itself depends on our life-state at each moment. At each moment we determine the future. As we experience Buddhahood more and more, the entire network of causes and effects which makes up our individual karma is dramatically transformed. Those things which induced suffering in the past work to enhance our development as human beings, now based on enlightenment rather than illusion.

Another important feature of the lotus is that it blooms from muddy swamps, showing that beauty can emerge from the darkest of places. In Nichiren Daishonin's Buddhism, we do not remove ourselves from the difficult realities of ordinary life. On the contrary, we plunge into them as a source of nutrition for our growth, just as the swamp nourishes the lotus flower. Naturally, the lotus does not reject the swamp because it is muddy. On the contrary, it thrives vigorously, 'enjoying' itself. Likewise, we enjoy our relationship with our environment when we are in the state of Buddhahood.

Kyo

Kyo means sutra, or teaching; it can also be interpreted to mean sound. Nichiren Daishonin said, '*Kyo* means the words and speech, sound and voices of all living beings'.[4] This indicates that the ultimate law to which the Buddha is enlightened is inherent in all living beings.

Kyo originally meant the warp of a length of cloth, summoning up the image of continuity. The Buddhist teachings are passed on through past, present and future. It therefore also means the eternity of life.

A Buddha's enlightenment is expressed through the voice of his teachings and the truth to which he is enlightened is eternal. Through chanting Nam-myoho-renge-kyo, we too become enlightened to this truth. We awaken to the eternal aspect of our own lives which transcends the changes of the physical world and the cycle of birth and death.

Nam

Nam is the way we relate to the law of Myoho-renge-kyo. *Nam* is derived phonetically from Sanskrit and is a word of invocation. Nichiren

Daishonin explains that it means the devotion of body and mind. When we chant, we concentrate both our bodies and minds.

Action is most important. Nam-myoho-renge-kyo contains many depths of meaning which we can study and which inspire us. However, it is the action of chanting which activates Buddhahood, even if we understand nothing. Nichiren Daishonin says:

> Those who chant Myoho-renge-kyo, the title of the Lotus Sutra, even without understanding its meaning, realise not only the heart of the Lotus Sutra, but also the essence of all the Buddha's teachings.[5]

Nam is a two-way communication. When chanting, we 'return' our lives to the unchanging eternal truth. We can then deal with the changing circumstances of life using the wisdom of Buddhahood. With this regular 'returning' rhythm, we are able to live based on our instrinsic enlightened nature.

There is nothing in our changing circumstances which is guaranteed to bring us lasting happiness. A career and a family can just as easily be sources of suffering as sources of joy. Enlightenment means that we are united with the rhythm of the entire universe, able to live with freedom and joy, whatever the uncertainties of our daily lives.

Myoho-renge-kyo is the king of sutras, flawless in both letter and principle. Its words are the reality of life, and the reality of life is the mystic law (*myoho*). It is called the mystic law because it explains the mutually inclusive relationship of life and all phenomena. That is why this sutra is the wisdom of all Buddhas.[6]

1 *The Major Writings of Nichiren Daishonin*, Vol. 1, p. 222.
2 *Major Writings*, Vol. 1, p. 5.
3 *Major Writings*, Vol. 7, pp. 65-6.
4 *Nichiren Daishonin Gosho Zenshu*, p. 708.
5 *Major Writings*, Vol. 3, p. 246.
6 *Major Writings*, Vol. 1, p. 3.

The
Gohonzon

'A mind which presently is clouded by illusions originating from the innate darkness of life is like a tarnished mirror, but once it is polished it will become clear, reflecting the enlightenment of immutable truth.'

What is the most important thing in our lives? Most people would agree that health is important. Many people put their family or loved one first. Others would say that their prime aim in life is to become successful in their careers. Lots of people want to be rich.

All of the above are highly desirable. However, there is something which is more desirable. That is a supremely fulfilled life-condition; a life filled with wisdom, confidence and caring, which is undisturbed by life's vicissitudes. Nichiren Daishonin inscribed the Gohonzon as the foundation for this kind of life.

Gohonzon literally means *hon* - foundation; *zon* - esteem; while *go* is an honorific prefix indicating respect. To practitioners of Nichiren Daishonin's Buddhism, the Gohonzon is the object of fundamental respect, or the object which we hold in highest esteem.

The problem with materialistic objects of devotion, such as careers or money, is that they are subject to change. If our happiness depends entirely on them, it is extremely fragile. If we do not become a millionaire, we are forever frustrated. If our loved one leaves, we are devastated.

Our objectives in life also determine the extent to which we can develop ourselves. If our objective is to make a million, this may make us determined and clever in business, but it will not develop, say, our appreciation of nature. Of course, most people would agree that there is more to life than making money. However, even if we dedicate ourselves, for example, to becoming a nurse devoted to helping others, a teacher, an inventor, or a good neighbour, the degree of both our development and our happiness is dependent on something which has limitations and is always subject to change.

The Gohonzon contains the enlightened life-condition of Buddhahood, which is unswayed by changing circumstances. The potential of human life in the Buddha state is limitless. When Nichiren Daishonin was alive, his followers could experience Buddhahood through their relationship with him. He left the Gohonzon for us so that we can be self-sufficient and practise to it to realize our own Buddhahood.

External objects have the power to change us, depending on our relationship to them. A painting can make us feel enraptured, disgusted, tranquil or perplexed, depending both on the mastery of the painter and on our responses to it. Money may also cause different reactions, mostly pleasure, but perhaps disgust if offered as a bribe. A letter received from a loved one will cause delight. A letter from the bank manager saying we are overdrawn may cause us anxiety.

The function of the Gohonzon is to enable us to draw forth our innate Buddhahood. The idea of an object of devotion may seem strange to western people. It may appear to be akin to idolatry. However, the Gohonzon is very different to an idol. We are not worshipping something superior or separate from ourselves. Rather, Nichiren Daishonin bequeathed us a graphic representation of the enlightened life-condition of the universe, the enlightened life-condition of our own lives. Through chanting Nam-myoho-renge-kyo, we fuse our lives with the Gohonzon and draw out and experience our own enlightened life-condition.

The use of an object as a focus of concentration for meditation is quite usual in Buddhism. It is called a mandala. Mandala is a Sanskrit word, originally meaning circle. In ancient India a circle was drawn in the sand around everyone taking part in religious ceremonies, signifying protection. A circle encompasses everything within it. It is all-embracing and therefore contains the meanings of universality, wholeness and healing; it encompasses the macrocosm and microcosm. The Gohonzon is also described as a 'cluster of blessings' and 'perfectly endowed'. Our lives are 'perfectly endowed' with everything we need for our happiness. Our innate Buddha nature responds to our chanting Nam-myoho-renge-kyo to the Gohonzon. Nichiren Daishonin encourages us to:

> Believe in this mandala with all your heart... I, Nichiren, have inscribed my life in *sumi* [ink], so believe in the Gohonzon with your whole heart.[1]

The Gohonzon is a scroll on which are written Chinese and Sanskrit characters. Written down the centre, in bold characters, is Nam-myoho-renge-kyo Nichiren. This signifies the oneness of the Law (Nam-myoho-renge-kyo) and the Person (Nichiren Daishonin). In other words,

Nichiren Daishonin's life was completely at one with the law of the universe. This qualified him to inscribe the ultimate truth.

On either side of this central inscription are written names of both historical and mythical figures who represent various functions of life. At the top, the historical Buddha, Shakyamuni, represents subjective wisdom and the mythical Buddha, Taho, represents objective reality. Also inscribed along the top are the names of four bodhisattvas who represent true self, eternity, purity and joy. These are all qualities of the state of Buddhahood.

All of the ten states of life (see p.21) appear on the Gohonzon, as well as various protective forces of the universe. Nichiren Daishonin explains:

Illuminated by the five characters of the Mystic Law [Myoho-renge-kyo], they display the enlightened nature they inherently possess. This is the true object of worship.[2]

This means that even seemingly negative life-states like hunger are transformed when one's life is based on Buddhahood. For example, hunger is represented by a mythical figure called Kishimojin. She was a female demon who had 500 children and, it is said, killed other people's babies to feed them to her own. She eventually became a believer in Buddhism and repented of her past misdeeds. Together with her children, she vowed to protect other believers. Kishimojin is inscribed quite low down on the Gohonzon. Hunger is an essential driving force and is therefore represented on the Gohonzon, like all other functions of life. If hunger dominates our lives - if it were written down the centre - it would be out of proportion and function negatively. In its correct perspective, and 'subservient' to Buddhahood, it functions to protect us.

There is a well-known phrase, 'looking at life through rose-tinted spectacles'. When people are in love, everything looks brighter and more beautiful than before. Life seems wonderful and easy. Other people respond to this, smiling fondly at young lovers. This is a good illustration of how both our perception of life and the environment change according to our life-state (in this case, rapture). We are all prone to particular basic states of life. If, for instance, we are dominated by anger, then everything in life is coloured by this and the environment responds accordingly - other people are angry towards us, or else avoid us.

When we chant to the Gohonzon, we are, as it were, putting our lives back in the right order, with the state of Buddhahood at the centre. Then everything responds to this enlightened state and functions to enhance and protect our lives. There are many external influences in daily life which bring out our lower life-conditions, such as hell or anger. The external stimulus for Buddhahood is the Gohonzon. This is why we need to regularly return to the Gohonzon and focus on Buddhahood.

Various forces of the universe, such as the sun and the moon, are also inscribed on the Gohonzon. These forces can be destructive as well as beneficial. The sun is essential to life and yet can burn and do great harm. When we chant to the Gohonzon, the forces of the universe function in a protective way because we are acting from our enlightened nature. Nichiren Daishonin wrote:

> Buddhism teaches that when the Buddha nature manifests itself from within, it will obtain protection from without. This is one of its fundamental principles.[3]

The Gohonzon is often described as a mirror. It is the mirror which reflects our greater self - the self of the enlightened human being, in harmony with universal life. We cannot see our own face without a mirror. Similarly, because our wisdom is limited, we cannot see our Buddhahood. When we face the mirror of the Gohonzon and chant Nam-myoho-renge-kyo, we can see through our illusions and discover the treasure of our own lives.

The Gohonzon embodies enlightened and eternal universal life. By making this our highest object of devotion, we are by no means cutting out other commitments. On the contrary, with the unlimited potential of the Gohonzon at the centre of our lives, we are able to take on many other commitments, but they do not dominate or overwhelm us because they are a part of the picture, not an end in themselves.

No matter what our objectives in life are, what every human being fundamentally desires is enlightenment. By drawing forth our Buddhahood in front of the Gohonzon, we tap the source of vitality that enables us to constantly refresh and invigorate ourselves. We also experience the eternal nature of our lives which gives us stability.

Practice to the Gohonzon is all about growth. Through repeatedly experiencing how we can turn difficult situations into benefit for our lives, we deepen the power of our faith. In this way, we build a life which is not dependent on outside circumstances; it is so strongly orientated towards our Buddha nature that nothing can make us feel defeated.

In earlier forms of Buddhism, people had to undertake many difficult and complicated practices over many lifetimes in order to arrive at an intuitive awakening to the ultimate truth. Nichiren Daishonin made this unnecessary by bequeathing us the ultimate truth in the form of the Gohonzon. Embracing and practising to the Gohonzon throughout our lives is in itself attaining Buddhahood. In fact, the emphasis of the practice of Nichiren Daishonin's Buddhism is to awaken Buddhahood in others. Daisaku Ikeda explains this:

> The teaching 'embracing the Gohonzon is itself enlightenment' represents a revolutionary view of what it means to attain Buddhahood. Mr Toda said, 'In contrast to the Buddhas of the "Expedient Means" Chapter [of the Lotus Sutra] who have practised for tens of millions of years, we can complete our practice for attaining Buddhahood by simply believing in the Gohonzon and chanting the single phrase Nam-myoho-renge-kyo'... We can attain this vast state of Buddhahood directly - right now - right where we are. Then we go out in society and tell others of the exhilaration we experience in manifesting this state of life. This practice represents the quintessence of the Daishonin's Buddhism.[4]

1 *The Major Writings of Nichiren Daishonin*, Vol. 1, pp. 119-20.
2 *Major Writings*, Vol. 1, p. 212.
3 *Major Writings*, Vol. 2, p. 233.
4 *Conversations and Lectures on the Lotus Sutra*, Vol. 1, p. 186.

The **Practice** *of* **Nichiren Daishonin's Buddhism**

'Arouse deep faith and polish your mirror night and day. How should you polish it? Only by chanting Nam-myoho-renge-kyo.'

Up to this point, we have looked at some of the basic principles of Nichiren Daishonin's Buddhism. There is nothing in his teachings which contradicts reason. However, the purpose of his life's work was to enable people to become supremely happy in themselves and contribute to a creative and peaceful world. He established the practice whereby anyone can do this.

The value of a theory is demonstrated by the effect it has when put into action. For example, a doctor's education is valuable when he uses his learning for the sake of healing others. In fact, we refer to a doctor as practising medicine. The word practice is used in the same way when applied to Buddhism.

Nichiren Daishonin's Buddhism entails practice for oneself and others. Practice for oneself is gongyo, which means assiduous practice. It is done morning and evening, and consists of chanting Nam-myoho-renge-kyo as well as reciting sections of the Lotus Sutra.

We recite two key chapters of the Lotus Sutra as preparation for the main practice of chanting Nam-myoho-renge-kyo. These are the 'Expedient Means' (second) chapter which teaches that all people have innate Buddhahood and 'The Life Span of the Thus Come One' (sixteenth) chapter which reveals the eternity of life. When we do gongyo, we are praising the magnificence and wonder of life and expressing our appreciation for it.

Gongyo is at the same time easy and difficult. Because it is easy, it is accessible to anyone. Because it is difficult, we can revolutionise our lives. This twice daily assiduous practice is what enables us to base our lives on Buddhahood, rather than our deluded natures. Because of this it can be a struggle. We have to get up earlier; it always seems there are more important things to do when we get home; when we sit down to do it, sometimes we really do not want to be there. This is the daily struggle to break the chains of our own destiny. It is always important to remember that we are doing it for no one but ourselves. This is our own opportunity to liberate ourselves from habitual behaviour which makes us suffer; to experience confidence, joy and freedom.

When we do gongyo, we leave behind our daily worries and devote time to ourselves. Before gongyo we may feel anxious or depressed, or short of time. During gongyo we experience the eternal, unchanging enlightened nature of the universe. We return our lives to the ultimate truth. After gongyo we can go about our tasks feeling refreshed. This twice daily rhythm is necessary in just the same way as we eat or sleep. Eating and sleeping refresh us physically and psychologically. Gongyo refreshes the universal self.

Practice for others means to introduce Nichiren Daishonin's teachings to others. This is important because it means taking action. The development of compassion is an essential aspect of our practice. In Buddhism, compassion (*jihi*) means to take away unhappiness and give happiness. It is not the same as charity, because charity usually means to take away unhappiness. Although this is valuable, it is far more valuable to give someone the means to change their lives for ever. We therefore teach people the Buddhism of Nichiren Daishonin. In fact, practice for others also benefits us, because we develop our compassion which is an enlightened quality. Similarly, gongyo is not solely for ourselves, but also benefits others as we chant for them and also master our own negative tendencies.

Study is also part of the practice for oneself and others. By studying the Buddhist teachings, we are able to explain the philosophy to others and also understand it ourselves. Study, in the Buddhist sense, is not academic learning but an aid to faith. In one of his writings, Nichiren Daishonin says:

> Exert yourself in the two ways of practice and study. Without practice and study, there can be no Buddhism. You must not only persevere yourself, you must also teach others. Both practice and study arise from faith. Teach others to the best of your ability... Nam-myoho-renge-kyo.[1]

As this passage says, there are three elements to Nichiren Daishonin's Buddhism - faith, practice and study. Faith in Buddhism does not mean blind belief or passive acceptance. It refers to that realm of life which lies beyond the intellect. When our limited thinking tells us that things are hopeless, faith opens our hearts to other possibilities. As Nichiren Daishonin says:

What we call faith is nothing extraordinary. As a woman cherishes her husband, as a man will give his life for his wife, as parents will not abandon their children, or as a child refuses to leave his mother, so should we put our trust in the Lotus Sutra [the Gohonzon] ... and chant Nam-myoho-renge-kyo.[2]

Faith is a natural quality of human life. We have faith that the sun will rise in the morning - in fact, we don't even think about it. But if we were to doubt all the things we take for granted in our daily lives, we would be living in a state of abject fear. Life would be terrible. In contrast, the more faith we have, the happier we are. We tend to think that faith means belief. However, when we start to practise, it is natural to have very little, if any, belief. More important than belief is a seeking mind. Our belief in the Gohonzon naturally grows as we experience the joy of practice.

In Buddhism, faith means a pure heart, a flexible spirit and an open mind. Faith is the function of human life to dispel the dark clouds of doubt, anxiety and regret, and sincerely open and direct one's heart towards something great. Faith might also be characterized as the power that enables the microcosm of the self to sense the universal macrocosm.[3]

Faith, it could be said, is the end result of practising. Absolute faith in the universal law of life - in ourselves, in others and in the universe - is the most open, secure and enjoyable state of life. Everyone wants this feeling of serenity, security and strength. In another sense, faith is the beginning, because without the ability to open our hearts to possibilities beyond our present experience, we would not be able to start practising.

There is a phrase in the first section of gongyo meaning 'bravely and vigorously' (*yu myo sho jin*):

Without such a brave and vigorous spirit, we cannot break the iron shackles of destiny, nor can we defeat obstacles and devils. Our daily practice of gongyo is a drama of challenging something new in our lives. When we bravely stand up with faith, the darkness of despair and anxiety vanishes from our hearts, and in pours the light of hope and growth. This spirit to stand up courageously is the spirit of faith.[4]

In this passage, 'obstacles and devils' refers to the resistance we meet when we try to move forwards. This is very natural. If we were to train as an athlete, we would get aches and pains in training. Other people also, when they see us trying to develop our lives, can feel threatened and try to stop us. At first, this may be off-putting. However, as our practice and faith become strong, we find that difficulties or opposition only serve to fuel our forward momentum. For example, when learning to ski, people avoid steep slopes. Expert skiers, however, relish the thought of difficult slopes and find them exhilarating.

When we practise Nichiren Daishonin's Buddhism we are training ourselves for life. We do not seek to avoid hardship, but to become so strong in ourselves so that we can handle anything. Nichiren Daishonin advises us:

Never let life's hardships disturb you. After all, no one can avoid problems, not even saints or sages.[5]

Furthermore, as we practise for ourselves and others, we are seeking to establish a peaceful and creative society. Naturally this is difficult and full of challenges. The practice of Nichiren Daishonin's Buddhism is in no way euphoric. We must always deal with the tangible reality which exists in front us. Only through dealing with reality can we prove the power of the Gohonzon in our own lives and for the sake of others. Only in this way can we change our destiny for the better:

In life, we must not permit ourselves to be absorbed only with immediate realities. We must have ideals and strive to achieve them, thereby transcending present realities. On the other hand, we must not allow ourselves to become alienated from reality. We can change nothing unless our feet are firmly planted on the ground.[6]

1 *The Major Writings of Nichiren Daishonin*, Vol. 1, p. 95.
2 *Major Writings*, Vol. 5, p. 303.
3 Daisaku Ikeda, *Conversations and Lectures on the Lotus Sutra*, Vol. 1, p. 177.
4 Daisaku Ikeda, *Conversations and Lectures on the Lotus Sutra*, Vol. 1, p. 187.
5 *Major Writings*, Vol. 1, p. 161.
6 Daisaku Ikeda, *Conversations and Lectures on the Lotus Sutra*, Vol. 1, p. 104.

Human Revolution *and* World Peace

'You must never seek any of Shakyamuni's teachings or the Buddhas and bodhisattvas of the universe outside yourself. Your mastery of the Buddhist teachings will not relieve you of mortal sufferings in the least unless you perceive the nature of your own life. If you seek enlightenment outside yourself, any discipline or good deed will be meaningless.'

W e tend to think that happiness is caused by something which comes from outside: something 'makes' us happy. The happiness we refer to in Buddhism is not dependent on outside events. Rather, true happiness comes about when we value our own Buddha nature. This requires a change from within, not without. This inner change is often referred to as 'human revolution' and is the objective of practising Nichiren Daishonin's Buddhism.

Our practice, in fact, has a two-fold aim. As well as the process of human revolution, we are working to establish *kosen-rufu*. This is often translated as world peace, but means much more than that. Literally, it is to 'widely declare and spread' the teachings of Buddhism. This aim goes far beyond the establishment of a world without war, although this is one aspect of it. *Kosen-rufu* means the widespread acceptance of Buddhist philosophy as the foundation of society.

The great Russian writer, Solzhenitsyn said:

The structure of the state is secondary to the spirit of human relations. Given human integrity, any honest system is acceptable, but given human rancour and selfishness, even the most sweeping of democracies will become unbearable. If the people themselves lack fairness and honesty, this will come to the surface under any system.[1]

This view perfectly accords with the Buddhist perception. Of course we can change the system or have an external revolution, but if the people in that system do not master themselves, the benefits of the change of system will be short-lived. This is why the inner, or human, revolution is so important.

Developments in science and technology have built a formidable body of knowledge which has led civilisation throughout the twentieth century. However, knowledge alone is incapable of leading us through periods of tumultuous and swift change such as we are now witnessing. We need wisdom:

Simply put, knowledge corresponds to the past; it is technology.

Wisdom is the future; it is philosophy. It is people's hearts that move the age. While knowledge may provide a useful point of reference, it cannot become a force to guide the future. By contrast, wisdom captivates people's hearts and has the power to open a new age.[2]

So how are we to gain this wisdom which is so desperately needed to bring about a peaceful and creative world? It is traditionally believed that wisdom comes from thought. However, Buddhism goes further, teaching that wisdom arises from caring: caring for the plight of other human beings, for the animal world and the future of our planet. To take a simple example, a mother who cares about her child naturally has the wisdom to know what to do when her baby is crying. If, however, she is overwrought, she may get angry or depressed. If so, she will not have the wisdom to deal with the problem and may well make it worse.

The source of the Buddha's wisdom is compassion. The Buddha's wisdom arises from and is at one with compassion. The Buddha's wisdom to perceive the nature of reality to the very core, arises from his strong and single-minded compassionate determination to save those who are suffering.[3]

The above quotation seems to be referring to one particular Buddha, but Nichiren Daishonin insists that everyone is a Buddha. We acknowledge this when we chant Nam-myoho-renge-kyo and take action to teach others about Buddhism. This is how we come to believe in our inherent wisdom: we experience it.

Buddhahood is a completely natural state. We feel calm and untroubled, concerned for the welfare of others and confident in our ability to take wise action. This kind of happiness does not depend on everything going well. It does not disappear when we encounter difficulties, because we understand the true nature of life. Being secure in our sense of oneness with the universe, and in the eternity of life, we are able to act with compassion and wisdom, with the utmost respect for all life. This enlightened life-condition brings an abiding sense of happiness and well-being.

This change in individual lives will bring about a profound effect in society. Historian Arnold Toynbee perceived that the way people respond to difficulties in their environment is a measure of their civilisation. He said that if people have developed the inner resources to react to calamity with a refusal to be defeated, they are able to emerge from disaster with dignity and optimism.

Dr Toynbee believed that even in instances where 'knowledge' hesitates and shrinks back, 'hope' courageously steps forward, advancing dauntlessly and infusing life with eternal brilliance. Hope is strength. Hope is born of courage and wisdom; it is not born of knowledge alone. And faith creates the wisdom that gives rise to boundless and eternal hope.[4]

A book called *The 900 Days: The Seige of Leningrad*[5], tells the stories of people who endured a two-and-a-half year ordeal. Amazingly, the author discovered that what sustained the people more than anything were radio transmissions of poetry and music. These broadcasts were important, too, for those musicians, readers and poets who made the great effort to respond to those trapped without much food or heat. The radio broadcasts gave great hope and nourished the spirits both of those who received and those who gave.

For too long we have imagined that our own feelings and opinions are unreliable and unimportant. In many ways, we have handed our lives over to experts or professionals who, we think, know better than we do. There are now many signs that people in various fields are recognising the importance of the subjective self. This change of emphasis is not confined to alternative medicine or religion.

Physicists and biologists have discovered that the mind informs and guides the intricate interactions of every cell in the body. Scientists who previously thought that reality was purely physical have now discovered that consciousness plays a crucial role in determining the physical self. It may be a long time yet before the prevailing scientific thinking, and therefore that of society, presents a balanced view of the interaction between consciousness and physical reality. However, as Buddhists, we establish this balance daily through our practice for ourselves and others.

Buddhist concepts clarify the true nature of life: the law of cause and effect; the interconnectedness of all life, sentient and insentient; equality, respect and the dignity of life. If society were to be based on these values, it would be a very different place. However, we do not have to wait for society to improve before establishing these values as the basis for our own lives. In fact, a healthy society depends on us doing this.

We can be happy and fulfilled amidst the turmoil and sufferings of our troubled times. As we each create this enlightened life-condition and influence our surroundings, the ripples spread outwards to create the kind of world we all want.

Establishing a peaceful society means overcoming prejudice and the desire to dominate others. However, we also have to overcome greed and short-term profit motives in order to sustain the natural environment. Legislation and political initiatives are not enough in themselves to establish this kind of world. The most important factor lies in the hearts of people.

For too long, it would seem, we have failed to acknowledge the vital role that the subjective self plays in our well-being, the wealth of positive, creative qualities within that we can nourish. We have also failed to acknowledge how a looked-for change in social and natural conditions depends on these resources.

Peace is not merely the absence of war; and peace is irrelevant if the planet is destroyed through pollution and waste of natural resources. The only certain way to achieve lasting peace and creative living is surely the human revolution, whereby each individual overcomes greed, hatred and narrow-mindedness, cultivating the treasures of the heart.

Real solutions to the environmental problems we face cannot be found on the political or economic level alone; we must dig down to grapple with the values that shape them on a deeper dimension. Buddhist teachings include an exquisite metaphor of the cosmic view of history, showing how all the phenomena of the universe interrelate, producing a perfect, delicate harmony. They also present the law of oneness of life and its environment (*esho funi*), which defines the dynamic pulsing of creative life that prevails between the subjective human life (*shoho*) and the objective environmental world (*eho*) that surrounds it. This law shares the same principle as expressed in the words of Spanish philosopher, Jose Ortega y Gasset: 'I am my environment. If that environment cannot be saved, I cannot be saved.' That is the reason the Soka Gakkai International has long aspired to achieve an 'environmental revolution' and a 'global revolution' through the medium of 'human revolution'.[6]

1 Aleksander Solzhenitsyn, *Rebuilding Russia: Reflections and Tentative Proposals*, p. 49.
2 Daisaku Ikeda, *Conversations and Lectures on the Lotus Sutra*, Vol. 2, p. 184.
3 Daisaku Ikeda, *Conversations and Lectures on the Lotus Sutra*, Vol. 2, pp. 184-5.
4 Daisaku Ikeda, 'Spreading the Philosophy of Great Compassion throughout the World', printed in *SGI-UK Guidance Booklet*, Vol. 11, p. 171.
5 Harrison E. Salisbury, *The 900 Days: The Seige of Leningrad*.
6 Daisaku Ikeda, *Peace Proposal 1997*.

The **Life** *of* **Nichiren Daishonin**

Nichiren Daishonin declared Nam-myoho-renge-kyo to be the ultimate law on 28 April 1253. Twenty-six years later, on 12 October 1279, he inscribed the Dai-Gohonzon, a great mandala dedicated to the happiness of all humankind. He died in 1282, having devoted his life to the study, reformation and propagation of Buddhism.

The young Zennichimaro (splendid sun), as he was named at birth, was born into extraordinarily turbulent times in Japan. Not only was there social unrest with fighting between rival warrior clans, there were also natural catastrophes such as the great earthquake which struck the capital, Kamakura, in 1257. To add to the problems, the Mongols were threatening to invade. Society was in disarray, as was the land, and Buddhist sects were confused about which of the many different teachings were correct.

It seems that Zennichimaro was a deep thinker from an early age. He was later to write, 'Since childhood, I, Nichiren have never prayed for the secular things of this life but have single-mindedly sought to become a Buddha.'[1] On another occasion he said:

Ever since my childhood I have studied Buddhism with one thought in mind. Life as a human being is pathetically fleeting. A man exhales his last breath with no hope to draw in another. Not even dew borne by the wind suffices to describe this transience. No one, wise or foolish, can escape death. My sole wish has therefore been to solve this eternal mystery. All else has been secondary.[2]

Zennichimaro was the son of a fisherman. His parents must have sensed his potential as they sent him to study at the local temple at the age of eleven. There, he prayed to become the wisest man in Japan. In response to his seeking mind, he became enlightened to the essential nature of life which enabled him to distinguish between truth and illusion. He set out to study all the Buddhist teachings from the age of fifteen, when he became a priest.

Shakyamuni, the founder of Buddhism in India, had predicted three time periods during which Buddhism would develop and change after his death. During the first thousand years, he said, people would be able to attain enlightenment through his teachings. In the second millenium, Buddhism would become dominated by ritual and formality, gradually losing its power to lead people to enlightenment. This duly happened around the sixth to ninth centuries AD when many temples were built in China and Japan.

According to the Japanese Buddhist tradition, the third period, known as the Latter Day of the Law, began in 1052. At this time, Shakyamuni had said, Buddhism would decline and a new teacher would appear to spread the true law, suitable for the people of that age, which would last 'ten thousand years and more'. The Buddhist sects of the time were therefore afraid that the attainment of Buddhahood would no longer be possible through their traditional methods of practice. New schools sprang up. The Jodo sect, also known as Nembutsu, was the most popular of these among the common people. It claimed that belief in a higher power was the only way to salvation and that chanting the name of a Buddha called Amida would enable rebirth in a Western Paradise, removed from this world. Zen also gained influence at this time, mostly among the warrior class. It advocated abandoning all the written texts and concentrating on personal effort under the guidance of a teacher. Both were attempts, though at opposite ends of the scale, to simplify Buddhist practices which had become extremely complex and beyond people's capability.

It was widely accepted at that time, as it probably was in

medieval Britain, that the actions and beliefs of the people were reflected in the environment. Thus, if people were practising the correct religion, they would expect to be rewarded with good weather, peace and harmonious social conditions. It was blatantly obvious that this was not the case in Japan, in these times of huge difficulties. These are described by Nichiren Daishonin in one of his writings:

> In recent years, there are unusual disturbances in the heavens, strange occurrences on earth, famine and pestilence, all affecting every corner of the empire and spreading throughout the land. Oxen and horses lie dead in the streets, the bones of the stricken crowd the highways. Over half the population has already been carried off by death, and in every family someone grieves.[3]

Nichiren Daishonin travelled extensively to study at all the temples which were centres of learning. He was confident, with his enlightened life-condition, that he could find documentary evidence for the correct Buddhist teaching for the Latter Day of the Law.

He returned after his travels to the temple of his education, Seicho-ji, and gave a lecture declaring Nam-myoho-renge-kyo (see p.79) to be the teaching for this time. It was then that he took the name Nichiren (sun-lotus). At the same time, he vociferously refuted the four prevalent Japanese Buddhist sects, which included Zen and Nembutsu. Because of this, he is sometimes described by other Buddhist sects as 'belligerent', or even 'militant', although he never bore arms. He was certainly full of conviction that Nam-myoho-renge-kyo, the heart of the Lotus Sutra, is the ultimate Buddhist teaching and the only way to enlightenment in this turbulent age of the Latter Day of the Law. He based his conclusions on documentary proof (the Lotus Sutra), theoretical proof (the study of doctrine) and actual proof (the fact that it works).

> A law this easy to embrace and this easy to practise was taught for the sake of all mankind in this evil age of the Latter Day of the Law.[4]

It is important to understand that Nichiren Daishonin's overriding concern was for the welfare of the people; he could see clearly that misleading philosophies lead to misery. His declaration that all people, equally, can attain Buddhahood here and now, deeply upset the priests and people in authority who wanted to retain their power. His denunciation of authorities which used people for their own misguided ends was unequivocal. However, one has only to read his letters to his followers to see that his compassion towards ordinary people was truly great.

His statements drew upon him a lifetime of persecutions. He knew, however, that he was carrying out his purpose in life as the Buddha of the Latter Day of the Law and fulfilling the predictions of Shakyamuni. These predictions were quite specific, detailing the persecutions which would befall the votary of the Lotus Sutra in the Latter Day of the Law, including exile on more than one occasion. Nichiren Daishonin was exiled twice: to the peninsula of Izu and to the island of Sado. Both banishments were meant to ensure his certain death. Nichiren Daishonin wrote, 'Had it not been for the advent of Nichiren in the Latter Day of the Law, the Buddha would have been a great liar.'[5] To Nichiren Daishonin, there was no greater happiness than to establish the universal law. The persecutions were an inevitable part of his purpose in life:

> I think I have practised the Lotus Sutra twenty-four hours each day and night. I say so because, having been exiled on the Lotus Sutra's account, I now read and practise it continuously whether I am walking, standing, sitting or lying down. For anyone born human, what greater joy could there be?[6]

Every time Nichiren Daishonin entered a debate with other sects, or wrote to the government, he was persecuted anew. Despite this, he continued the propagation of Nam-myoho-renge-kyo and won many followers. They, too, were subjected to harassment by the authorities. The most serious was the Atsuhara Persecution, when twenty peasant-farmers were arrested and tortured in an attempt to make them give up their faith. They refused. Three of them were later executed. Because of their strong faith, Nichiren Daishonin knew he could rely on his disciples to protect the law in the future. It was then that he inscribed the Dai-Gohonzon, dedicated to the happiness of all humankind, the fulfilment of his lifelong purpose. Thanks to him, and the fortitude of his disciples, the ultimate law for this age has survived and been passed down to this day.

Now in the second year of Koan (1279), it is twenty-seven years since I first proclaimed the true teaching at Seicho-ji temple ... The Buddha fulfilled the purpose of his advent in a little over forty years; T'ien-t'ai took about thirty years, and Dengyo, some twenty years. I have repeatedly spoken of the indescribable persecutions they suffered during those years. For me it took twenty-seven years and the persecutions I faced during this period are well known to you all.[7]

1 *The Major Writings of Nichiren Daishonin*, Vol. 3, pp. 238-9.
2 *Nichiren Daishonin Gosho Zenshu*, p. 1404.
3 *Major Writings*, Vol. 2, p. 3.
4 *Major Writings*, Vol. 1, p. 222.
5 *Major Writings*, Vol. 1, p. 240.
6 *Major Writings*, Vol. 5, p. 7.
7 *Major Writings*, Vol. 1, p. 239.

Soka Gakkai International

Soka Gakkai International (SGI) is a worldwide movement dedicated to peace, education and culture based on the Buddhism of Nichiren Daishonin. Soka means value-creation and Gakkai means society. The international society was formed in 1975 in response to an increasing worldwide membership. This had grown from the original Soka Kyoiku Gakkai (Value-creating Education Society) founded in Japan by the educator Tsunesaburo Makiguchi (1871-1944) in 1930.

Makiguchi was passionately concerned with humanistic education. In addition to writing about education, he also published a book entitled *The Philosophy of Value*. It is the creation of value, he said, that enables people to establish happiness and become fulfilled. He met Nichiren Daishonin's Buddhism in 1928 and recognised it as the most effective philosophy and practice for creating value, based on universal concepts and the utmost respect for life. The society he established gradually grew from a group concerned solely with education, to involve people from all walks of life interested in practising Nichiren Daishonin's Buddhism.

During the Second World War, the militaristic government in Japan tried to enforce allegiance to the Emperor and the war effort by coercing people into accepting Shintoism as the state religion. Makiguchi refused to compromise the teachings of Nichiren Daishonin. For this, he was imprisoned in 1943. Despite torture and interrogation, he refused to renounce his Buddhist faith and died in Tokyo Detention House on 18 November 1944.

Josei Toda, who regarded Makiguchi as his mentor in life, was also imprisoned. He survived and was released in July 1945. Despite his weak physical condition, he immediately set about reconstructing the lay organisation, renaming it the Soka Gakkai. The membership had collapsed under the government restrictions, so he started again with a burning desire for peace and the happiness of all people. He condemned nuclear weapons as 'an absolute evil that threatens the people's right of existence'. Under his leadership, the movement grew to more than 750,000 households by the time of his death in 1958.

Daisaku Ikeda became president of the Soka Gakkai in 1960 and immediately devoted himself to fulfilling Toda's aspiration for the worldwide propagation of Nichiren Daishonin's teachings. There are now over ten million members in Japan as well as around a million in 128 other countries.

Before the advent of the Soka Gakkai, Nichiren Daishonin's Buddhism was little known. This was partly because of government ideology. Freedom of religion was not established in Japan until after the Second World War. Moreover, the teachings were spread little outside a small number of priests and their families.

Josei Toda introduced the idea that lay believers should practise Buddhism as Nichiren Daishonin had taught; that is, practice for oneself and others, and study of the Daishonin's writings. Toda started a new movement for lay believers centred on reciting gongyo twice daily, reading and discussing Nichiren Daishonin's letters and treatises, and propagating his teachings. Until then, it was the Japanese custom that lay believers simply made donations to the temples and the priests conducted ceremonies on their behalf.

Toda also brought into the light of day those writings of Nichiren Daishonin that had been preserved. These writings exist mostly in the form of letters to followers and the Soka Gakkai published his collected writings in 1952. Toda began the widespread propagation of these unique teachings which had until then been known only to a tiny sect.

Josei Toda's wisdom was such that he recognised that erroneous philosophies lead people in the direction of suffering. This was particularly apparent in the Second World War, when the Japanese state religion led to unbelievable barbarism and horror. The teachings of Nichiren Daishonin are based on the utmost respect for life. They clarify the universal law as Nam-myoho-renge-kyo, thereby providing a means for people to revolutionise their lives, overcome suffering and create value for themselves and others.

Toda was very close to the retired fifty-ninth high priest of Nichiren Shoshu, Nichiko Hori, and they worked together on the compilation of Nichiren Daishonin's writings. As the membership of the Soka Gakkai grew, the mutually supportive relationship with the successive high priests at the Head Temple, Taiseki-ji, continued. However, since 1980, when Nikken became high priest, the Nichiren Shoshu priesthood has become increasingly unable to open itself to the needs of a diverse and international membership.

Practising Nichiren Daishonin's Buddhism only as a formality, and becoming rich and powerful through the donations of SGI members, the priesthood came to consider itself infallible. In direct opposition to Nichiren Daishonin's teachings of equality, the high priest placed himself in a superior position to other believers. In 1991, Nikken excommunicated the entire SGI membership in an attempt to destroy the movement altogether. This act is unprecedented in the whole religious history of the human race. However, although many members have undoubtedly been confused by this, it has released the movement from the constraints of authoritarianism. SGI is now able to flourish even more in its secular role of contributing to peace, education and culture in concert with like-minded people.

SGI's activities are based on the belief that inner reformation, or human revolution, is the key to creating a peaceful world. As Daisaku Ikeda says:

Nichiren Daishonin, the thirteenth century Buddhist sage, whose teachings we at SGI follow said, 'Life itself is the most precious of all treasures'[1]. This respect for life is the essential inspiration of the Toda declaration [against nuclear weapons]. Herein lies the reason we at SGI aspire for the inner revolution of all individuals - the human revolution - that will establish the respect for all life as the basic norm of human society. Life is the world's supreme treasure. There is no value that is worth preserving at the sacrifice of life. The human revolution movement is the basis upon which SGI has held various exhibitions (such as 'Nuclear Arms: Threat to Our World' and 'War and Peace'), designed to raise awareness of nuclear and other global issues. Through these activities we have worked to expand a network of solidarity among people worldwide.[2]

In addition to the exhibitions mentioned above, SGI has co-sponsored conferences and staged exhibitions on environmental and human rights issues: for example, in support of the 1992 Earth Summit, and the forty-fifth anniversary of the United Nations' adoption of the Universal Declaration of Human Rights.

The SGI is a non-governmental organisation registered with the United Nations, pledging itself to the pacifist principles on which it is founded. SGI conducts many fund-raising and relief activities in support of refugees all over the world.

In addition to activities for peace, SGI promotes education and culture, recognising their vital role in the development of the unique creative potential of each individual. In Japan there are Soka schools at kindergarten, elementary, and high school level. There are also universities in Tokyo and Los Angeles. These are devoted to nurturing people of wisdom and humanity who will contribute to the realisation of a peaceful world. Special emphasis is given to respect for the natural environment, appreciation of diverse cultures and traditions, and the development of a global outlook. To this end, there are extensive exchange programmes between Soka University and other universities worldwide. There is no religious instruction included in the curriculum and admission is open to students without regard to religious affiliation.

There are numerous other educational programmes. The Institute of Oriental Philosophy was established in 1962 and has centres in India, Hong Kong, Russia and the UK. The Boston Research Centre and Toda Peace Institute foster human rights, inter-religious and cultural understanding, and promote co-operation in the building of a peaceful future.

Exchanges between people of different cultures as a celebration of their diversity is also undertaken through the Min-on Concert Association, which stages a vast range of music and dance. The Fuji Art Museum, founded in 1983 with the motto 'a museum creating bridges around the world', and the Victor Hugo House of Literature, established in Paris in 1991, also promote international dialogue through literature and the arts.

The fundamental role of the SGI, however, is always to provide a basis for the practice, study and propagation of Nichiren Daishonin's Buddhism. Members study and discuss the application of Buddhist principles to daily life at monthly meetings to which guests are welcome. These are the backbone of all other activities. In the UK there are currently about six thousand members in local districts throughout the country. The national centre is based at Taplow Court in Buckinghamshire.

The co-ordination of such a diverse range of activities is possible through a very particular kind of unity. Unlike many organisations, no conformity is required. Individuals are able to give full play to their particular characters and abilities. Unity is based on each person's commitment to human revolution and the creation of a peaceful world.

1 *The Major Writings of Nichiren Daishonin*, Vol. 1, p. 267.
2 Daisaku Ikeda, *Peace Proposal* 1997.

Charter of the Soka Gakkai International

We, the constituent organisations and members of the Soka Gakkai International (SGI), embrace the fundamental aim and mission of contributing to peace, culture and education based on the philosophy and ideals of the Buddhism of Nichiren Daishonin.

We recognise that at no other time in history has humankind experienced such an intense juxtaposition of war and peace, discrimination and equality, poverty and abundance as in the twentieth century; that the development of increasingly sophisticated military technology, exemplified by nuclear weapons, has created a situation where the very survival of the human species hangs in the balance; that the reality of violent ethnic and religious discrimination presents an unending cycle of conflict; that humanity's egoism and intemperance have engendered global problems, including degradation of the natural environment and widening economic chasms between developed and developing nations, with serious repercussions for humankind's collective future.

We believe that Nichiren Daishonin's Buddhism, a humanistic philosophy of infinite respect for the sanctity of life and all-encompassing compassion, enables individuals to cultivate and bring forth their inherent wisdom and, nurturing the creativity of the human spirit, to surmount the difficulties and crises facing humankind and realise a society of peaceful and prosperous co-existence.

We, the constituent organisations and members of SGI, therefore, being determined to raise high the banner of world citizenship, the spirit of tolerance, and respect for human rights based on the humanistic spirit of Buddhism, and to challenge the global issues that face humankind through dialogue and practical efforts based on a steadfast commitment to non-violence, hereby adopt this Charter, affirming the following:

Purposes and Principles

1 SGI shall contribute to peace, culture and education for the happiness and welfare of all humanity, based on the Buddhist respect for the sanctity of life.

2 SGI, based on the ideal of world citizenship, shall safeguard fundamental human rights and not discriminate against any individual on any grounds.

3 SGI shall respect and protect the freedom of religion and religious expression.

4 SGI shall promote an understanding of Nichiren Daishonin's Buddhism through grass-roots exchange, thereby contributing to individual happiness.

5 SGI shall, through its constituent organisations, encourage its members to contribute towards the prosperity of their respective societies as good citizens.

6 SGI shall respect the independence and autonomy of its constituent organisations in accordance with the conditions prevailing in each country.

7 SGI shall, based on the Buddhist spirit of tolerance, respect other religions, engage in dialogue and work together with them towards the resolution of fundamental issues concerning humanity.

8 SGI shall respect cultural diversity and promote cultural exchange, thereby creating an international society of mutual understanding and harmony.

9 SGI shall promote, based on the Buddhist ideal of symbiosis, the protection of nature and the environment.

10 SGI shall contribute to the promotion of education, in the pursuit of truth as well as development of scholarship, to enable all people to cultivate their characters and enjoy fulfilling and happy lives.

Daisaku Ikeda

D aisaku Ikeda has been working for peace as president of the Soka Gakkai since 1960. Born in 1928, he grew up during the Second World War and witnessed his four older brothers being drafted into military service. The eldest was killed in action. In one of his essays, he recalls his awareness of his mother's suffering at the loss of her son. He became acutely aware of the suffering that war causes to ordinary people everywhere.

He met Josei Toda at the age of nineteen and immediately recognised in him a man of peace and hope. Toda had total conviction in the power of the Buddhism of Nichiren Daishonin to enable people to become happy. He had the knack of being able to explain profound Buddhist concepts in a straightforward logical manner.

Ikeda came to regard Toda as his mentor in life and learned about Buddhism, as well as many other subjects, through his guidance. He took a fully supportive role in the effort to establish Nichiren Daishonin's Buddhism in Japan after the Second World War. Ikeda became president of the Soka Gakkai two years after Toda's death.

Josei Toda's goal of establishing a membership of 750,000 households was achieved before his death. He had also dreamt of spreading the Buddhism of Nichiren Daishonin overseas, which he was never able to do himself. However, Ikeda immediately began to travel the world, starting with the USA in 1960, determined to fulfil his mentor's vision of a peaceful world.

Although Ikeda was never a school teacher like Toda, his efforts for peace have always been based on the broadest of educational principles: the full development of each individual human being. He constantly encourages people, particularly young people, to study and develop their own thoughts as well as their creativity. In the case of members, this is based on faith in Nichiren Daishonin's Buddhism. However, he also lectures at universities throughout the world, bringing a message of hope, which underlies the practical solutions to the world's problems.

Since 1983, Ikeda has presented an annual Peace Proposal giving practical suggestions as to how to solve such world problems as disarmament and the protection of the environment. He carries out an extraordinary number of dialogues with world leaders and philosophers on Buddhist concepts as applied to peace, culture and education in today's world. He does this in addition to his main role of providing inspiration and insight for the SGI's membership. Many of his speeches, dialogues and guidances are published.

Ikeda writes prolifically, his most notable work perhaps being *The Human Revolution*, a twelve-volume novel telling the history of the Soka Gakkai since 1945. *The New Human Revolution* starts in 1960 when he assumed the presidency. The foreword to the series records the now famous sentence:

A great revolution of character in just a single individual will help achieve a change in the destiny of a nation, and further, will cause a change in the destiny of humankind.[1]

1 *The Human Revolution*, (1961) p. iii.

Further Reading

RICHARD CAUSTON, The Buddha in Daily Life: An Introduction to the Buddhism of Nichiren Daishonin.
London: Rider, 1995, 299pp.
This is an accessible introduction to the teachings and practice of Nichiren Daishonin's Buddhism. It covers subjects such as faith, the ten worlds, the Gohonzon, and Soka Gakkai International. It also provides a comprehensive explanation of Nam-myoho-renge-kyo. Throughout the work there are examples of the ways in which individuals have used their Buddhist practice to overcome obstacles and to fulfil their potential in all areas of life.

DAISAKU IKEDA, Unlocking the Mysteries of Birth and Death: Buddhism in the Contemporary World.
London: Warner, 1995, 218pp.
This work examines the issues of birth, longevity, sickness, and death. It illuminates the correspondence between Buddhist thought and concepts in modern science. It also explains Nam-myoho-renge-kyo, the nine consciousnesses and *ichinen sanzen* (three thousand realms in a single life-moment).

DAISAKU IKEDA, Dialogue on Life, Vols. 1 & 2.
Tokyo: NSIC, 1995, 243pp & 268pp.
Wide-ranging discussions on various aspects of life from the viewpoint of Buddhist philosophy. Volume One contains topics such as body and mind, self-identity and man in nature. Volume Two includes perhaps the most far-reaching discussion yet published on the subject of life and death.

ARNOLD TOYNBEE AND DAISAKU IKEDA, Choose Life: A Dialogue.
Oxford: Oxford University Press, 1976, 374pp.
In this dialogue on personal, social, political, philosophical and religious life, the authors discuss issues of urgent concern for the future. Despite wide differences between the authors' cultural and religious backgrounds, their dialogue brings to light a remarkable degree of agreement; notably their conviction that the spiritual search of individuals is the only sure way of creating a lasting improvement in society.

JOHAN GALTUNG AND DAISAKU IKEDA, Choose Peace: A Dialogue Between Johan Galtung and Daisaku Ikeda.

London: Pluto Press, 1995, 172pp. Discussing Buddhism and peace, the authors highlight sources of global violence and unrest. They offer positive, practical proposals as an approach to social and political issues such as nationalism, fundamentalism, the death penalty, arms reduction and the role of the United Nations in peace-keeping initiatives.

BRYAN WILSON AND DAISAKU IKEDA, Human Values in a Changing World: A Dialogue on the Social Role of Religion.

New York: L. Stuart, 1988, 364pp. The authors share their thoughts on social topics and their relationship to ethical and religious values. The subjects under discussion include the concept of sin, sexual ethics, euthanasia, genetic engineering, the future of the family, authority and democracy, and community values.

AURELIO PECCEI AND DAISAKU IKEDA, Before It Is Too Late: A Dialogue Between Aurelio Peccei and Daisaku Ikeda.

London; Sydney: Macdonald, 1984, 192pp. The authors discuss the wide-ranging global crises confronting humankind today. Whilst acknowledging the enormous benefits and opportunities that have resulted from advances in science and technology, the authors believe that, essentially, today's gravest problems stem from a spiritual and ethical malaise which is immune to both science and economics. From their different perspectives, the authors argue that long-term solutions will only be found as more and more individuals commit themselves to a profound renewal of their vision and values.

LINUS PAULING AND DAISAKU IKEDA, A Lifelong Quest for Peace: A Dialogue.

Boston; London: Jones & Bartlett, 1992, 118pp. The authors seek to provide pointers to help young people solve the problems of the twenty-first century. Written in a very personal way, they discuss issues such as disarmament, international understanding and peace.

BRYAN WILSON AND KAREL DOBBELAERE, A Time to Chant: The Soka Gakkai Buddhists in Britain.
Oxford: Oxford University Press, 1994, 267pp.

This objective analysis of SGI-UK is based on the responses of more than six hundred members to a wide-ranging questionnaire and thirty loosely structured interviews with members. The findings cover all aspects of members' practice and faith including how they met Nichiren Daishonin's Buddhism, what particularly attracted them to it, the benefits they get from it, and their commitment to SGI. In addition the study examines members' values and attitudes to life. Although a control group was not used in this analysis, the authors (neither of whom is affiliated with SGI) do compare members' responses with data provided by the UK sample of the European Value Study (1990).

DAISAKU IKEDA, A New Humanism: The University Addresses of Daisaku Ikeda.
New York; Tokyo: Weatherhill, 1994, 224pp.

Twenty-two speeches and lectures given by the author at universities, research institutes and academies around the world on the themes of culture, art, education and peace.

DAISAKU IKEDA, A Lasting Peace, Vols. 1 & 2.
New York; Tokyo: Weatherhill, 1981 & 1987, 272pp & 300pp.

These volumes contain a collection of Daisaku Ikeda's speeches and proposals concerning peace, education and culture. They include addresses given at universities in Europe and the United States, presenting Buddhist concepts as applied to daily life and world problems. They also contain some of his Peace Proposals to the United Nations.

DAISAKU IKEDA, The Human Revolution.
[to be completed in 12 volumes] Taplow, Bucks: SGI-UK, 1994- .

This novel describes the growth of the Soka Gakkai in post-war Japan under the organisation's second president, Josei Toda. He was a man who lived with the single-minded conviction that 'a great revolution of character in just a single individual will help achieve a change in the destiny of a nation and, further, will cause a change in the destiny of all humankind.' As well as history, it contains many practical explanations of Buddhist philosophy.

DAISAKU IKEDA, The New Human Revolution.
[On-going series.] Taplow, Bucks: SGI-UK, 1995-.
These volumes portray the growth of Soka Gakkai International throughout the world since 1960. It is the author's belief that this record of the expansion of the movement for *kosen-rufu* since President Toda's death will most truly illustrate his mentor's vision and the validity of Nichiren Daishonin's teachings today. It contains many personal experiences illustrating how Buddhism applies to daily life.

DAISAKU IKEDA, The Living Buddha: An Interpretive Biography.
New York; Tokyo: Weatherhill, 1996, 148pp.
This biography not only portrays the life and character of Shakyamuni, but also examines the nature of the Dharma or truth to which he was enlightened, and discusses whether it is accessible to others.

The Life of Nichiren Daishonin.
Tokyo: NSIC, 1996, 129pp.
This account of Nichiren Daishonin's life vividly illustrates his lifelong struggle to establish the Buddhism of the Latter Day of the Law. The work contains numerous references to the Daishonin's own writings (Gosho), since these letters and treatises provide the best sources for understanding his development, his endeavours and his conviction.

The Major Writings of Nichiren Daishonin, Vols. 1-7.
Tokyo: NSIC.
English translations of the *Gosho Zenshu* (Collected Writings) of Nichiren Daishonin (1222-1282). Currently available in seven volumes containing 172 letters and treatises.

Note: NSIC and SGI-UK publications are available only through SGI-UK outlets. For mail order, please send s.a.e. to Mail Order Dept, SGI-UK, Taplow Court, Taplow, near Maidenhead, Berkshire, SL6 OER.

Glossary

Bodhisattva: The ninth of the ten states. A state characterised by compassion in which one dedicates oneself to saving others.

Buddha: An enlightened person.

Buddhahood: The highest of the ten states, characterised by boundless wisdom and infinite compassion.

Daimoku: Literally, the title of a sutra. Used to refer to Nam-myoho-renge-kyo.

Dai-Gohonzon: The Gohonzon which Nichiren Daishonin inscribed on 12 October 1279, 'bestowed upon all the world'.

Gohonzon: The concrete expression of the Law of Nam-myoho-renge-kyo in the form of a mandala. *Honzon* means 'object of fundamental respect'; *go* means 'worthy of honour'.

Gongyo: Literally, 'assiduous practice'. The twice daily practice of believers in Nichiren Daishonin's Buddhism. It consists of the recitation of a section from the second chapter, and the entire sixteenth chapter of the Lotus Sutra, followed by the chanting of Nam-myoho-renge-kyo.

Gosho: The writings of Nichiren Daishonin.

Human Revolution: The concept that a profound change in the depths of an individual's life effects a change in the social and natural environment.

Ichinen sanzen: 'Three thousand realms in a single life-moment'. A philosophical concept formulated by T'ien-t'ai based on the Lotus Sutra. At each moment, life experiences one of the ten states. Each of these ten states possesses the potential for all ten within itself, thus making one hundred possible states. Each of these hundred states possesses the ten factors, thus becoming one thousand states. Each of these possesses the three realms of existence, thus totalling three thousand realms.

Jihi: 'To remove unhappiness and give happiness.' The Buddhist definition of compassion.

Karma: The accumulation of causes and effects, lying deep within life, which exert an often unseen influence over the present and future.

Kosen-rufu: Literally, 'to widely declare and spread [Buddhism]'. This expression appears in the twenty-third chapter of the Lotus Sutra. Nichiren Daishonin indicates that Nam-myoho-renge-kyo is the Law to be declared and spread widely in the Latter Day of the Law.

Latter Day of the Law: The period beginning two thousand years after the death of Shakyamuni, when he predicted his teachings would lose their power. It is said to last ten thousand years and more. Buddhists in Nichiren Daishonin's day considered that the Latter Day of the Law began in AD 1052.

Lotus Sutra: The ultimate teaching of Shakyamuni, where he reveals the eternity of life and that everyone has the potential to become a Buddha. It consists of twenty-eight chapters.

Maka Shikan: 'Great Concentration and Insight'. One of T'ien-t'ai's three major works. It elucidates the principle of *ichinen sanzen*, based on the Lotus Sutra.

Mandala: Literally 'circle', it implies wholeness, universality, healing and protection. Used to describe the Gohonzon, it means 'perfectly endowed' or 'cluster of blessings'.

Mystic Law: (Jp. *Myoho*) The ultimate law of life and the universe, the law of Nam-myoho-renge-kyo.

Nam-myoho-renge-kyo: Literally, 'Devotion to the Sutra of the Lotus Blossom of the Wonderful Law'. The ultimate Law or absolute reality permeating all phenomena in the universe, according to Nichiren Daishonin. (For full explanation see p.79).

Nichiren Daishonin (1222-1282): The Buddha of the True Cause who first declared Nam-myoho-renge-kyo to be the ultimate Law of the universe on 28 April 1253.

Nirvana: In the Theravadin sutras, to attain enlightenment by extinguishing earthly desires and escaping the cycle of birth and death. In Nichiren

Daishonin's Buddhism, nirvana means an enlightened condition of life in the real world.

Seven kinds of gems: These appear in the Treasure Tower (eleventh) chapter of the Lotus Sutra, decorating the tower. They are gold, silver, lapis lazuli, giant clam shell, coral, pearl and carnelian. They represent aspects of Buddhist practice: listening to the teaching, believing it, embracing it, meditating on it, practising it assiduously, devoting oneself to it, and always reflecting on oneself and working towards self-improvement.

Shakyamuni: Also known as Siddhartha Gautama. The first historically recorded Buddha who lived in India. Opinions differ as to exactly when he lived. Some sources say he lived around 400 or 500 BC. Contemporaries of Nichiren Daishonin placed the dates of his life at 1029-949BC as recorded in *Zhou Shu Yi Ji* (Record of Wonders in the Book of Zhou), an ancient Chinese text.

Soka Gakkai: Society for the creation of value, founded in 1930.

Taho: A Buddha who appears seated within the Treasure Tower at the Ceremony in the Air to attest to the validity of Shakyamuni's teaching. This takes place in the eleventh chapter of the Lotus Sutra.

Ten Factors: Also referred to as the 'ten suchnesses'; aspects common to all of the ten states. Mentioned in the

second chapter of the Lotus Sutra, they
are: appearance, nature, entity, power,
influence, inherent cause, external
cause or relation, latent effect, manifest
effect and consistency from beginning
to end.

Ten States: Ten potential conditions
of life. They are hell, hunger, animality,
anger, tranquillity, rapture, learning,
realisation, bodhisattva and
Buddhahood.

Ten Worlds: See Ten States.

Three Realms: Classified by
T'ien-t'ai, they are (1) The realm of
self, consisting of the five components -
form, perception, conception, volition
and consciousness; (2) The realm of
sentient beings; (3) The realm of the
natural environment.

Three Thousand Realms: See
Ichinen Sanzen.

T'ien-t'ai (538-597): Also known as
Chih-i. He formulated the concept of
ichinen sanzen.

Bibliography

The full references for the works quoted are given below:

DAISAKU IKEDA, Conversations and Lectures on the Lotus Sutra.
Taplow, Bucks: SGI-UK. Vol. 1, 1995. Vol. 2, 1996. Vol. 3, 1998.

DAISAKU IKEDA, The Human Revolution, Vol. 1.
Tokyo: The Seikyo Press, 1961.

DAISAKU IKEDA, A Lasting Peace, Vol. 1.
New York; Tokyo: Weatherhill, 1981.

DAISAKU IKEDA, Life: An Enigma, a Precious Jewel.
New York: Kodansha, 1986.

DAISAKU IKEDA, A New Humanism.
New York: Weatherhill, 1995.

DAISAKU IKEDA, 'Spreading the Philosophy of Great Compassion throughout the World'.
Printed in *SGI-UK Guidance Booklet*, Vol.11, 1996.

The Major Writings of Nichiren Daishonin.
Tokyo: NSIC. Vol. 1, 1979. Vol. 2, 1995. Vol. 3, 1985. Vol. 4, 1986. Vol. 5, 1988. Vol. 7, 1994.

Nichiren Daishonin Gosho Zenshu (Collected Writings - Japanese edition).
Tokyo: Soka Gakkai, 1952.

HARRISON E. SALISBURY, The 900 Days: The Seige of Leningrad.
London: Secker & Warburg, 1969.

ALEKSANDER SOLZHENITSYN, Rebuilding Russia: Reflections and Tentative Proposals.
London: Harvill, 1991.

Toda Josei Zenshu (The Collected Works of Josei Toda).
Tokyo: Seikyo Shimbunsha, 1985.

ARNOLD TOYNBEE & DAISAKU IKEDA, Choose Life: A Dialogue.
Oxford: Oxford University Press, 1989.

The Lotus Sutra trans. Burton Watson.
New York: Columbia University Press, 1993.

For further information please contact
SGI-UK
Taplow Court, Taplow
Near Maidenhead
Berkshire SL6 0ER
Tel: 01628 773163